Diabetic Diet After 50:

1900+ Days of Easy, Low-Carb, Low-Sugar Healthy Recipes – The Complete Cookbook with Delicious Food and 30-Day Meal Plan for Senior Diabetics and Health-Conscious Individuals.

Jakob Stivenson

2024

Table Of Contents

Disclaimer: The information contained in this cookbook is for educational and informational purposes only and is not intended as health or medical advice. The recipes and advice provided are based on the personal experience and research of the author, Jakob Stivenson, but are not a substitute for professional medical guidance. Always seek the advice of your physician or other qualified health provider with any questions you may have regarding a medical condition or dietary changes.

The author and publisher disclaim any liability for any adverse effects resulting directly or indirectly from information contained in this book. While efforts have been made to ensure the accuracy of the information presented, the author and publisher make no representations or warranties of any kind, express or implied, about the completeness, accuracy, reliability, suitability, or availability with respect to the content contained within this cookbook for any purpose. Any reliance you place on such information is therefore strictly at your own risk.

The author and publisher assume no responsibility for errors or omissions or for any consequences from the application of the information contained in this book and expressly disclaim all liability for any damages, loss, or risk, whether personal or otherwise, which is incurred as a consequence, directly or indirectly, of the use and application of any of the contents of this book.

Biography of Jakob Stivenson

Hi, I'm Jakob Stivenson, a chef, author, and passionate advocate for diabetic-friendly cooking. My love for cooking began at a young age, inspired by my mother and grandmother, who were exceptional home cooks. Growing up in their kitchen, I developed a deep appreciation for the joy and creativity of preparing meals.

My culinary journey took a personal turn when my sister was diagnosed with type 2 diabetes. Witnessing her struggle with dietary restrictions and the impact on her quality of life deeply affected me. Determined to help her and others in similar situations, I dedicated myself to honing my cooking skills and developing the best recipes for people with diabetes. My mission has always been to prove that managing diabetes doesn't mean sacrificing flavor or enjoyment.

For many years, I researched, experimented, and refined my recipes, focusing on low-sugar, low-carb, and low-fat ingredients that are still bursting with flavor. My latest work, " Diabetic Diet After 50:1900+ Days of Easy, Low-Carb, Low-Sugar Healthy Recipes – The Complete Cookbook with Delicious Food and 30-Day Meal Plan for Senior Diabetics and Health-Conscious Individuals." is a culmination of these efforts. This cookbook offers a comprehensive guide to managing diabetes with delicious, easy-to-prepare meals, and includes a 30-day meal plan specifically designed for senior diabetics and health-conscious individuals.

Throughout my career, I have been privileged to help countless individuals manage their diabetes through better nutrition. Hearing how my cookbooks have made a difference in their lives is incredibly rewarding and fuels my passion to continue creating and sharing. My vision is to show that people with diabetes can live full, vibrant lives with a normal, delicious diet.

Join me on this culinary journey. Together, we can redefine what it means to eat well and live well with diabetes. Explore my cookbook, try my recipes, and discover how you can transform your health one meal at a time.

Jakob Stivenson – Redefining Diabetic-Friendly Cooking, One Recipe at a Time

Introduction

Brief introduction to the book's purpose.

Welcome to "Diabetic Diet After 50:1900+ Days of Easy, Low-Carb, Low-Sugar Healthy Recipes – The Complete Cookbook with Delicious Food and 30-Day Meal Plan for Senior Diabetics and Health-Conscious Individuals." This cookbook is designed with you in mind, offering a wealth of recipes and dietary guidance tailored specifically for seniors managing diabetes. As we age, maintaining a balanced and nutritious diet becomes increasingly crucial, especially for those dealing with the unique challenges posed by diabetes.

This book's purpose is to provide you with practical, delicious, and easy-to-prepare meals that are low in sugar, carbohydrates, and fat, helping you to manage your blood sugar levels effectively while enjoying a variety of flavors. With over 1900 days' worth of recipes, you'll discover an extensive range of meal options that ensure you never have to sacrifice taste for health.

In addition to recipes, this cookbook offers valuable insights into the fundamentals of a diabetic-friendly diet, tips for meal planning, and strategies for maintaining a healthy lifestyle. Our goal is to empower you with the knowledge and tools necessary to make informed dietary choices, improve your overall health, and enhance your quality of life.

Embark on this culinary journey with us and discover how easy and enjoyable healthy eating can be, even with diabetes. Let's make every meal a step towards better health and well-being.

Importance of a Healthy Diet for Senior Diabetics

Maintaining a healthy diet is crucial for everyone, but it becomes especially vital for senior diabetics. As we age, our bodies undergo various changes that can affect how we process food and regulate blood sugar levels. For those with diabetes, these changes can make managing the condition more challenging. Here are some key reasons why a healthy diet is essential for senior diabetics:

1. Blood Sugar Control

A well-balanced diet helps regulate blood sugar levels, which is critical for managing diabetes. Consuming foods that are low in sugar and carbohydrates prevents spikes in blood glucose, reducing the risk of complications associated with diabetes, such as heart disease, kidney damage, and nerve issues.

2. Weight Management

Maintaining a healthy weight is important for controlling diabetes. Excess weight can increase insulin resistance, making it harder to manage blood sugar levels. A diet rich in low-calorie, nutrient-dense foods can help seniors achieve and maintain a healthy weight, thereby improving their overall health.

3. Nutrient Intake

As we age, our nutritional needs change. Seniors require more of certain nutrients to maintain bone health, muscle mass, and immune function. A diet that includes a variety of fruits, vegetables, lean proteins, and whole grains ensures that senior diabetics get the essential vitamins and minerals they need to stay healthy.

4. Reduced Risk of Complications

A healthy diet can help reduce the risk of diabetes-related complications. Foods that are high in fiber, healthy fats, and lean protein can improve cardiovascular health, lower cholesterol levels, and reduce blood pressure, all of which are important for minimizing the risk of heart disease and stroke in diabetics.

5. Improved Energy Levels

Eating a balanced diet helps maintain steady energy levels throughout the day. This is particularly important for seniors, as fluctuations in energy can affect their ability to stay active and engaged in daily activities. Consuming regular, balanced meals and snacks can help prevent energy slumps and promote a more active lifestyle.

6. Enhanced Quality of Life

Ultimately, a healthy diet contributes to a better quality of life. When senior diabetics follow a diet that supports their health, they are more likely to feel better physically and mentally. This can lead to greater independence, improved mood, and a more positive outlook on life.

In summary, a healthy diet is a cornerstone of effective diabetes management for seniors. By making informed food choices, senior diabetics can control their blood sugar levels, maintain a healthy weight, and reduce the risk of complications, all of which contribute to a higher quality of life and overall well-being.

Understanding Diabetes

Overview of Diabetes and Its Impact on Health

Diabetes is a chronic medical condition characterized by high levels of glucose (sugar) in the blood. It occurs when the body either cannot produce enough insulin or cannot effectively use the insulin it produces. Insulin is a hormone produced by the pancreas that helps regulate blood sugar levels by facilitating the entry of glucose into cells, where it is used for energy. There are three main types of diabetes: Type 1, Type 2, and gestational diabetes.

Types of Diabetes

1. **Type 1 Diabetes**
   - **Description:** An autoimmune condition where the body's immune system attacks and destroys the insulin-producing beta cells in the pancreas.
   - **Onset:** Typically diagnosed in children and young adults, though it can occur at any age.
   - **Management:** Requires daily insulin injections or an insulin pump to manage blood glucose levels.
2. **Type 2 Diabetes**
   - **Description:** The most common form of diabetes, where the body becomes resistant to insulin or does not produce enough insulin.
   - **Onset:** Generally develops in adults over the age of 45, but increasingly seen in younger populations due to rising obesity rates.
   - **Management:** Often managed through lifestyle changes such as diet and exercise, along with oral medications or insulin therapy.

3. **Gestational Diabetes**
    - o **Description:** A temporary form of diabetes that occurs during pregnancy when the body cannot produce enough insulin to meet increased needs.
    - o **Onset:** Develops during pregnancy and typically resolves after childbirth.
    - o **Management:** Managed through diet, exercise, and sometimes insulin or medication. Women with gestational diabetes are at higher risk of developing Type 2 diabetes later in life.

Impact on Health

Diabetes can have far-reaching effects on overall health, particularly when blood sugar levels are not well-managed. Long-term complications of diabetes can affect multiple organ systems and lead to serious health issues, including:

1. **Cardiovascular Disease**
    - o Diabetes significantly increases the risk of heart disease and stroke. High blood sugar levels can damage blood vessels and the nerves that control the heart and blood vessels.
2. **Neuropathy**
    - o Prolonged high blood sugar can cause nerve damage, particularly in the legs and feet. This can lead to pain, tingling, and loss of sensation, increasing the risk of injuries and infections.
3. **Kidney Damage (Nephropathy)**
    - o Diabetes can damage the delicate filtering system of the kidneys, leading to chronic kidney disease or even kidney failure, which may require dialysis or a kidney transplant.
4. **Eye Damage (Retinopathy)**
    - o High blood sugar levels can damage the blood vessels in the retina, potentially leading to blindness. Diabetes also increases the risk of other eye conditions such as cataracts and glaucoma.
5. **Foot Problems**
    - o Nerve damage and poor blood flow can lead to serious foot problems, including ulcers and infections that may require amputation in severe cases.
6. **Skin Conditions**
    - o Diabetes can make individuals more susceptible to skin infections and other skin conditions, including bacterial and fungal infections.
7. **Mental Health**
    - o The chronic nature of diabetes and the constant management it requires can contribute to mental health issues such as depression, anxiety, and stress.

Managing Diabetes

Effective management of diabetes involves a combination of lifestyle changes, medication, and regular monitoring of blood sugar levels. Key components include:

- **Healthy Diet:** Eating a balanced diet that is low in sugar, carbohydrates, and unhealthy fats while rich in fiber, lean protein, and healthy fats.
- **Regular Exercise:** Engaging in regular physical activity to help maintain healthy blood sugar levels, improve cardiovascular health, and manage weight.
- **Medication:** Taking prescribed medications or insulin as directed by a healthcare provider.
- **Monitoring:** Regularly checking blood glucose levels to ensure they remain within target ranges.
- **Regular Check-Ups:** Visiting healthcare providers for routine check-ups to monitor and manage any complications.

In summary, diabetes is a serious chronic condition that requires careful management to prevent complications and maintain overall health. Understanding its impact on the body and adopting effective management strategies can help individuals with diabetes lead healthier, more fulfilling lives.

Importance of Diet in Managing Diabetes

Diet plays a pivotal role in the management of diabetes. The food choices you make can have a profound impact on your blood sugar levels, overall health, and quality of life. For individuals with diabetes, following a well-planned, balanced diet is essential for controlling the condition and preventing complications. Here are several key reasons why diet is so important in managing diabetes:

1. Blood Sugar Regulation

One of the primary goals in managing diabetes is to maintain blood sugar levels within a target range. Diet directly influences blood sugar levels. Consuming carbohydrates, for example, causes blood sugar to rise, while proteins and fats have a slower, more gradual effect. By choosing the right types of foods and carefully monitoring carbohydrate intake, individuals can better control their blood sugar levels and avoid dangerous spikes and dips.

2. Weight Management

Being overweight or obese is a significant risk factor for developing Type 2 diabetes and can make diabetes management more challenging. A healthy diet helps with weight loss and maintenance, which can improve insulin sensitivity and make it easier to manage blood sugar levels. For those with Type 2 diabetes, even a modest weight loss can significantly improve blood sugar control and reduce the need for medication.

3. Heart Health

Diabetes increases the risk of heart disease and stroke. A heart-healthy diet, low in saturated fats, trans fats, cholesterol, and sodium, can help reduce this risk. Incorporating more fruits, vegetables, whole grains, and healthy fats, such as those found in nuts and fish, supports cardiovascular health and can lower cholesterol levels and blood pressure.

4. Prevention of Complications

A balanced diet rich in nutrients can help prevent or delay the onset of diabetes-related complications, such as neuropathy (nerve damage), nephropathy (kidney damage), and retinopathy (eye damage). Foods high in antioxidants, vitamins, and minerals support overall health and protect against oxidative stress and inflammation, which are common in diabetes.

5. Enhanced Energy Levels

Consuming a balanced diet with appropriate portions of carbohydrates, proteins, and fats can help maintain stable energy levels throughout the day. This is particularly important for people with diabetes, as fluctuating blood sugar levels can lead to feelings of fatigue or weakness. Eating regular meals and snacks helps keep energy levels consistent and supports daily activities and physical exercise.

6. Improved Mood and Mental Health

Diet can also affect mental health and mood. Stable blood sugar levels are associated with better mood and cognitive function. Conversely, large fluctuations in blood sugar can lead to mood swings, irritability, and difficulty concentrating. A nutritious diet can help stabilize these levels, promoting better mental well-being and reducing the risk of depression and anxiety, which are more common in individuals with diabetes.

7. Building Healthy Habits

Adopting a healthy diet helps establish long-term habits that contribute to overall well-being. Learning to read food labels, understanding portion sizes, and making informed food choices become second nature and support a sustainable, healthy lifestyle. These habits not only help manage diabetes but also enhance overall health and prevent other chronic conditions.

Practical Tips for a Diabetes-Friendly Diet

- **Monitor Carbohydrate Intake:** Keep track of the type and amount of carbohydrates consumed. Opt for complex carbs, such as whole grains, legumes, and vegetables, which have a slower impact on blood sugar.
- **Incorporate Fiber:** High-fiber foods help control blood sugar levels and support digestive health. Include plenty of fruits, vegetables, and whole grains.
- **Choose Lean Proteins:** Protein helps manage blood sugar levels and supports muscle health. Choose lean meats, fish, poultry, tofu, and legumes.
- **Healthy Fats:** Include sources of healthy fats, such as avocados, nuts, seeds, and olive oil, which support heart health.
- **Limit Added Sugars and Refined Carbs:** Avoid sugary drinks, sweets, and highly processed foods that can cause rapid spikes in blood sugar.
- **Stay Hydrated:** Drink plenty of water and limit sugary beverages and excessive caffeine.
- **Regular Meals and Snacks:** Eat regular, balanced meals and healthy snacks to maintain stable blood sugar levels throughout the day.

In summary, diet is a cornerstone of diabetes management. By making informed food choices and adopting a balanced, nutritious diet, individuals with diabetes can effectively control their blood sugar levels, reduce the risk of complications, and improve their overall health and quality of life.

Benefits of a Healthy Diet After 50

Health Benefits for Seniors

As we age, maintaining a healthy diet becomes increasingly important for promoting overall well-being and quality of life. For seniors, proper nutrition can play a crucial role in preventing chronic diseases, enhancing physical and mental health, and improving longevity. Here are some key health benefits of a nutritious diet for seniors:

1. Improved Cardiovascular Health

A heart-healthy diet rich in fruits, vegetables, whole grains, and lean proteins can help lower cholesterol levels and blood pressure, reducing the risk of heart disease and stroke. Foods high in fiber, such as oats and legumes, and healthy fats, like those found in fish and nuts, are particularly beneficial for cardiovascular health.

2. Better Bone Health

As we age, bone density decreases, increasing the risk of osteoporosis and fractures. A diet rich in calcium and vitamin D is essential for maintaining strong bones. Dairy products, leafy green vegetables, and fortified foods are excellent sources of these nutrients. Additionally, weight-bearing exercises and proper nutrition can help preserve bone health.

3. Enhanced Immune Function

A balanced diet supports a robust immune system, helping seniors fight off infections and illnesses more effectively. Nutrient-rich foods, such as fruits, vegetables, nuts, and seeds, provide essential vitamins and minerals like vitamin C, vitamin E, and zinc, which play vital roles in immune function.

4. Weight Management

Maintaining a healthy weight is crucial for seniors, as being overweight or underweight can lead to various health problems. A well-balanced diet that is rich in nutrients and moderate in calories helps seniors achieve and maintain a healthy weight. Proper portion control and regular physical activity are also important components of weight management.

5. Better Digestive Health

A diet high in fiber promotes healthy digestion and can prevent common digestive issues such as constipation and diverticulosis. Fiber-rich foods, such as whole grains, fruits, and vegetables, aid in maintaining regular bowel movements and support a healthy gut microbiome.

6. Cognitive Health

Proper nutrition is linked to better cognitive function and a lower risk of cognitive decline and dementia. Diets rich in antioxidants, omega-3 fatty acids, and other brain-boosting nutrients support brain health. Foods like berries, fatty fish, nuts, and leafy greens have been shown to benefit cognitive function and memory.

7. Enhanced Mental Health

Eating a balanced diet can also positively affect mental health. Nutrient-dense foods help regulate mood and reduce the risk of depression and anxiety. Omega-3 fatty acids, found in fish and flaxseeds, and antioxidants, found in fruits and vegetables, play key roles in maintaining mental well-being.

8. Increased Energy Levels

A nutritious diet provides the necessary fuel for the body to function optimally. Consuming a variety of nutrient-rich foods ensures that seniors have sufficient energy to engage in daily activities, stay physically active, and maintain an overall sense of vitality.

9. Better Management of Chronic Conditions

For seniors managing chronic conditions such as diabetes, hypertension, and arthritis, a healthy diet is crucial. Proper nutrition can help control blood sugar levels, reduce inflammation, and manage blood pressure, contributing to better overall management of these conditions.

10. Longevity and Quality of Life

Overall, a healthy diet contributes to longevity and enhances the quality of life. By providing the body with essential nutrients, a balanced diet helps seniors stay active, independent, and engaged in their communities.

Good nutrition supports physical health, mental well-being, and emotional resilience, all of which are important for aging gracefully.

Practical Tips for Healthy Eating for Seniors

- **Eat a Variety of Foods:** Include a wide range of fruits, vegetables, whole grains, lean proteins, and healthy fats in your diet to ensure you get all the necessary nutrients.
- **Stay Hydrated:** Drink plenty of water throughout the day. Dehydration can be a common issue among seniors, so it's important to stay hydrated.
- **Mind Portion Sizes:** Pay attention to portion sizes to avoid overeating and to help manage weight.
- **Limit Added Sugars and Salt:** Reduce the intake of foods high in added sugars and salt to lower the risk of diabetes and hypertension.
- **Plan Balanced Meals:** Aim to include a mix of macronutrients (carbohydrates, proteins, and fats) in each meal to keep energy levels stable and support overall health.
- **Consult a Healthcare Professional:** Regularly check in with a healthcare provider or a registered dietitian to tailor dietary choices to individual health needs and conditions.

In conclusion, a healthy diet is a cornerstone of well-being for seniors. By making nutritious food choices, seniors can improve their physical health, mental clarity, and emotional well-being, leading to a more vibrant and fulfilling life.

Basics of a Diabetic Diet

Key Principles

Low-Sugar, Low-Carb, and Low-Fat Diabetic Diet Fundamentals

Managing diabetes effectively often involves making specific dietary adjustments to help control blood sugar levels, maintain a healthy weight, and reduce the risk of complications. A diet that is low in sugar, low in carbohydrates, and low in fat can be particularly beneficial for diabetics. Here are the fundamentals of such a diet:

1. Low-Sugar Diet

Reducing sugar intake is crucial for managing blood glucose levels. High sugar consumption can lead to rapid spikes in blood sugar, which is particularly harmful for individuals with diabetes. Here are some key principles of a low-sugar diet:

- **Avoid Added Sugars:** Limit foods and beverages with added sugars, such as sodas, candies, pastries, and many processed foods. Instead, opt for natural sources of sweetness, like fruits, but in moderation.
- **Read Labels:** Learn to read nutrition labels to identify hidden sugars. Ingredients like high fructose corn syrup, dextrose, and maltose are all forms of sugar.
- **Choose Whole Foods:** Focus on whole, unprocessed foods that do not contain added sugars. Fresh vegetables, whole grains, and lean proteins are excellent choices.
- **Natural Sweeteners:** If you need to sweeten foods, consider using natural sweeteners like stevia or monk fruit, which have minimal impact on blood sugar levels.

2. Low-Carb Diet

Carbohydrates have the most significant impact on blood sugar levels. Managing carb intake is essential for diabetics to maintain stable blood glucose levels. Here are some guidelines for a low-carb diet:

- **Count Carbs:** Be mindful of the amount of carbohydrates consumed at each meal. Work with a dietitian or use a carb-counting app to track your intake.
- **Choose Complex Carbs:** When consuming carbohydrates, opt for complex carbs such as whole grains, legumes, and vegetables. These foods have a lower glycemic index and provide more sustained energy.
- **Avoid Refined Carbs:** Limit refined carbohydrates like white bread, white rice, and sugary cereals. These can cause rapid increases in blood sugar levels.
- **Portion Control:** Pay attention to portion sizes to avoid consuming too many carbs in one sitting. Small, frequent meals can help maintain more stable blood sugar levels.

3. Low-Fat Diet

While fat is an essential nutrient, it's important for diabetics to focus on the type and amount of fat consumed. A low fat diet can help manage weight and reduce the risk of heart disease, which is a common complication of diabetes. Here are the basics of a low-fat diet:

- **Limit Saturated and Trans Fats:** Reduce intake of saturated fats found in red meat, full-fat dairy products, and fried foods. Avoid trans fats found in many processed and packaged foods.

- **Choose Healthy Fats:** Incorporate healthy fats from sources like avocados, nuts, seeds, and olive oil. These fats can improve heart health and help manage blood sugar levels.
- **Watch Portions:** Even healthy fats should be consumed in moderation. Fat is calorie-dense, and excessive intake can lead to weight gain.
- **Cook Wisely:** Use cooking methods that require less fat, such as grilling, baking, steaming, or poaching, instead of frying.

Combining Low-Sugar, Low-Carb, and Low-Fat

Combining these dietary principles can help create a balanced and effective diet for managing diabetes. Here are some practical tips:

- **Balanced Meals:** Aim to include a balance of lean proteins, complex carbohydrates, and healthy fats in each meal. For example, a meal could consist of grilled chicken (lean protein), quinoa (complex carb), and a side of steamed vegetables with olive oil (healthy fat).
- **Meal Planning:** Plan your meals and snacks ahead of time to ensure they meet your dietary goals. This can help you avoid last-minute, unhealthy choices.
- **Healthy Snacking:** Choose snacks that align with your dietary principles, such as a handful of nuts, a piece of fruit, or vegetable sticks with hummus.
- **Hydration:** Drink plenty of water throughout the day. Avoid sugary drinks and limit high-calorie beverages like juice and soda.

In conclusion, a diet that is low in sugar, low in carbohydrates, and low in fat is an effective strategy for managing diabetes. By making informed food choices and focusing on whole, unprocessed foods, individuals with diabetes can maintain stable blood sugar levels, manage their weight, and reduce the risk of complications. This approach to eating supports overall health and well-being, contributing to a higher quality of life.

Importance of Balanced Meals

Balanced meals are fundamental to maintaining overall health and well-being, especially for individuals managing chronic conditions such as diabetes. A balanced meal includes a variety of foods that provide essential nutrients your body needs to function optimally. Here are several reasons why balanced meals are so important:

1. Blood Sugar Control

For diabetics, maintaining stable blood sugar levels is crucial. Balanced meals that include appropriate portions of carbohydrates, proteins, and fats help prevent spikes and crashes in blood sugar levels. Carbohydrates are the primary source of energy, but they must be paired with proteins and healthy fats to slow down digestion and glucose absorption, resulting in more stable blood sugar levels.

2. Nutrient Intake

A balanced meal ensures that you receive a wide range of essential nutrients, including vitamins, minerals, fiber, and antioxidants. Each food group offers different nutrients that support various bodily functions. For example, fruits and vegetables provide vitamins and antioxidants, whole grains supply fiber, and proteins contribute to muscle repair and immune function. Ensuring a variety of nutrients helps prevent deficiencies and supports overall health.

3. Energy Levels

Consuming balanced meals throughout the day helps maintain steady energy levels. Carbohydrates provide immediate energy, while proteins and fats offer sustained energy. This balance prevents the highs and lows in energy that can result from consuming meals that are too high in refined carbs or sugars. Steady energy levels enable you to stay active, focused, and productive throughout the day.

4. Weight Management

Balanced meals can aid in weight management by providing the right amount of calories and nutrients without excess. Including a variety of food groups in each meal helps you feel satisfied and reduces the likelihood of overeating. Additionally, balanced meals that include fiber-rich foods promote satiety, helping you feel fuller for longer and reducing the temptation to snack on unhealthy options.

5. Digestive Health

Meals that include a mix of fiber, proteins, and healthy fats support digestive health. Fiber, found in fruits, vegetables, and whole grains, aids in regular bowel movements and prevents constipation. A healthy digestive system improves nutrient absorption and overall health.

6. Mental and Emotional Well-Being

Nutrition has a direct impact on brain health and mood. Balanced meals that provide a steady supply of glucose to the brain support cognitive function and help maintain concentration and alertness. Additionally, nutrients such as omega-3 fatty acids, found in fish and flaxseeds, and vitamins like B-complex vitamins, found in whole grains and leafy greens, are associated with improved mood and reduced symptoms of depression and anxiety.

7. Preventing Chronic Diseases

Balanced meals that include a variety of nutrient-dense foods can help reduce the risk of developing chronic diseases such as heart disease, hypertension, and certain cancers. For diabetics, balanced meals that are low in refined sugars and unhealthy fats can help manage the condition and prevent complications. Antioxidants and anti-inflammatory compounds found in fruits, vegetables, nuts, and seeds play a role in protecting the body from oxidative stress and inflammation, which are underlying factors in many chronic diseases.

8. Better Eating Habits

Consistently consuming balanced meals can help establish healthy eating patterns that are sustainable in the long term. This approach to eating encourages mindful eating, portion control, and the inclusion of a wide range of foods, leading to better overall dietary habits and improved health outcomes.

Nutritional Guidelines

Essential Nutrients for Diabetics

Proper nutrition is a key component in managing diabetes effectively and promoting overall health. Certain nutrients are particularly important for individuals with diabetes as they play crucial roles in regulating blood sugar levels, supporting metabolic processes, and preventing complications. Here are some essential nutrients for diabetics and their benefits:

1. Fiber

- **Benefits:** Fiber helps to slow down the absorption of sugar, which improves blood sugar control. It also supports digestive health and promotes a feeling of fullness, aiding in weight management.
- **Sources:** Whole grains (such as oats, brown rice, and whole wheat), fruits, vegetables, legumes (such as beans and lentils), nuts, and seeds.

2. Omega-3 Fatty Acids

- **Benefits:** Omega-3 fatty acids have anti-inflammatory properties and are beneficial for cardiovascular health. They help reduce the risk of heart disease, a common complication in diabetics.
- **Sources:** Fatty fish (such as salmon, mackerel, and sardines), flaxseeds, chia seeds, walnuts, and fish oil supplements.

3. Magnesium

- **Benefits:** Magnesium plays a crucial role in glucose metabolism and improving insulin sensitivity, which can help with blood sugar control.
- **Sources:** Leafy green vegetables (such as spinach and kale), nuts (such as almonds and cashews), seeds (such as pumpkin and chia), whole grains, and legumes.

4. Chromium

- **Benefits:** Chromium is a trace mineral that enhances the action of insulin and helps improve blood sugar control.
- **Sources:** Broccoli, barley, oats, green beans, tomatoes, and meat.

5. Vitamin D

- **Benefits:** Vitamin D is important for bone health and immune function. Some studies suggest that adequate vitamin D levels may improve insulin sensitivity and glucose control.
- **Sources:** Sunlight exposure, fatty fish (such as salmon and mackerel), fortified dairy products, egg yolks, and vitamin D supplements.

6. Antioxidants

- **Benefits:** Antioxidants help combat oxidative stress and inflammation, which are linked to diabetes complications. Vitamins C and E are notable antioxidants that can protect cells from damage.
- **Sources:** Fruits (such as berries, citrus fruits, and kiwi), vegetables (such as bell peppers, spinach, and broccoli), nuts, seeds, and green tea.

7. Potassium

- **Benefits:** Potassium helps regulate blood pressure and fluid balance in the body. Maintaining healthy blood pressure is important for reducing the risk of cardiovascular complications in diabetics.
- **Sources:** Bananas, oranges, sweet potatoes, tomatoes, spinach, and avocados.

8. Zinc

- **Benefits:** Zinc is involved in insulin production and secretion. Adequate zinc levels can support proper immune function and wound healing, which are critical for diabetics.
- **Sources:** Meat, shellfish, legumes, seeds, nuts, and whole grains.

9. Vitamin B Complex

- **Benefits:** B vitamins, including B1 (thiamine), B6 (pyridoxine), and B12 (cobalamin), play essential roles in energy metabolism and nerve function. They can help manage symptoms of diabetic neuropathy and support overall health.
- **Sources:** Whole grains, meat, eggs, dairy products, legumes, seeds, and nuts.

10. Protein

- **Benefits:** Protein helps maintain muscle mass, supports tissue repair, and promotes satiety, which can help with weight management and blood sugar control.
- **Sources:** Lean meats (such as chicken and turkey), fish, eggs, dairy products, tofu, legumes, and nuts.

Practical Tips for Incorporating Essential Nutrients

- **Balanced Diet:** Aim to include a variety of nutrient-rich foods in your daily diet to ensure you get all essential nutrients. Focus on whole foods rather than processed options.
- **Portion Control:** Be mindful of portion sizes to avoid overeating and ensure a balanced intake of nutrients.
- **Diverse Food Sources:** Rotate different foods within each nutrient category to benefit from the full range of vitamins and minerals they offer.
- **Supplements:** If you have difficulty meeting your nutritional needs through diet alone, consider discussing supplements with your healthcare provider.

In conclusion, ensuring an adequate intake of essential nutrients is vital for diabetics to manage their condition effectively and maintain overall health. By incorporating a variety of nutrient-dense foods into your diet, you can support blood sugar control, reduce the risk of complications, and enhance your quality of life.

Portion Control and Meal Timing

Effective diabetes management involves not only choosing the right foods but also paying close attention to portion sizes and meal timing. Proper portion control and regular meal timing can help maintain stable blood sugar levels, prevent overeating, and promote overall health. Here's how these strategies can benefit individuals with diabetes:

Portion Control

Portion control is essential for managing blood sugar levels and maintaining a healthy weight. Here are some key points about portion control:

1. Understanding Portion Sizes

- **Measuring Portions:** Use measuring cups, spoons, or a food scale to ensure you're consuming the right portion sizes. Familiarize yourself with standard serving sizes for different food groups.
- **Visual Cues:** Use visual references to estimate portion sizes. For example, a serving of meat or fish should be about the size of a deck of cards, while a serving of cooked vegetables should fit in the palm of your hand.

2. Benefits of Portion Control

- **Blood Sugar Stability:** Smaller, controlled portions can help prevent spikes and dips in blood sugar levels. Consistent portions lead to more predictable blood sugar responses.
- **Weight Management:** Controlling portion sizes helps in managing calorie intake, which is crucial for maintaining or achieving a healthy weight. Excess weight can increase insulin resistance, making diabetes management more challenging.
- **Better Digestion:** Smaller, more frequent meals are easier for the body to digest and can help prevent digestive discomfort.

3. Practical Tips for Portion Control

- **Plate Method:** Use the plate method to create balanced meals. Fill half your plate with non-starchy vegetables, one-quarter with lean protein, and one-quarter with whole grains or starchy vegetables.
- **Mindful Eating:** Eat slowly and pay attention to hunger and fullness cues. Avoid distractions such as watching TV while eating, which can lead to overeating.
- **Pre-Portioned Snacks:** Choose pre-portioned snacks to avoid overeating. For example, divide nuts into small bags or buy single-serving containers of yogurt.

Meal Timing

Consistent meal timing helps regulate blood sugar levels and supports metabolic health. Here are some important aspects of meal timing:

1. Regular Meal Schedule

- **Consistent Timing:** Try to eat meals and snacks at the same times each day. Consistency helps your body anticipate and manage blood sugar levels more effectively.
- **Balanced Meals:** Ensure each meal is balanced with a mix of carbohydrates, proteins, and fats to sustain energy levels and prevent blood sugar spikes.

2. Frequency of Meals

- **Multiple Small Meals:** Consider eating smaller, more frequent meals throughout the day rather than three large meals. This approach can help maintain stable blood sugar levels and reduce hunger.
- **Scheduled Snacks:** Incorporate healthy snacks between meals to keep blood sugar levels steady. Choose snacks that include protein and fiber, such as an apple with peanut butter or a handful of almonds.

3. Timing Around Physical Activity

- **Pre-Exercise Nutrition:** If you plan to exercise, eat a small meal or snack that includes carbohydrates about 30 minutes to an hour before your workout to prevent low blood sugar during exercise.

- **Post-Exercise Nutrition:** After exercise, have a snack or meal that includes protein and carbohydrates to replenish energy stores and aid in muscle recovery.

Practical Tips for Meal Timing

- **Plan Ahead:** Plan your meals and snacks in advance to ensure you eat regularly and have healthy options available. Preparing meals ahead of time can help you avoid last-minute unhealthy choices.
- **Avoid Skipping Meals:** Skipping meals can lead to overeating later in the day and can cause blood sugar fluctuations. Make it a priority to eat at regular intervals.
- **Nighttime Eating:** Be mindful of eating late at night. Consuming large meals right before bed can lead to higher blood sugar levels in the morning.

Portion control and meal timing are critical components of effective diabetes management. By understanding portion sizes and maintaining a regular eating schedule, individuals with diabetes can better control their blood sugar levels, manage their weight, and improve overall health. Implementing these strategies requires mindful planning and consistency but can lead to significant improvements in diabetes management and quality of life.

How to Read and Understand Food Labels

Reading and understanding food labels is a crucial skill for managing diabetes and making informed dietary choices. Food labels provide valuable information about the nutritional content of a product, helping you choose foods that support your health goals. Here's a guide to help you navigate food labels effectively:

1. Serving Size

- **Definition:** The serving size is the amount of food that is considered one serving. All the nutritional information on the label is based on this serving size.
- **Importance:** Pay attention to the serving size and compare it to the amount you actually eat. If you consume more or less than the serving size, you'll need to adjust the nutritional values accordingly.

2. Calories

- **Definition:** Calories measure the amount of energy provided by the food.
- **Importance:** Monitoring calorie intake is essential for weight management. Ensure that the calories per serving fit into your daily caloric needs.

3. Total Carbohydrates

- **Definition:** This includes all the carbohydrates in one serving of the food, including fiber, sugars, and starches.
- **Importance:** Carbohydrates have the most significant impact on blood sugar levels. Pay close attention to the total carbohydrate content to manage your carb intake effectively.

4. Dietary Fiber

- **Definition:** Fiber is a type of carbohydrate that the body cannot digest. It helps regulate blood sugar levels and supports digestive health.
- **Importance:** Foods high in fiber are beneficial for diabetics. Aim for products with higher fiber content to help control blood sugar and improve satiety.

5. Sugars

- **Definition:** This includes both naturally occurring sugars and added sugars in the food.
- **Importance:** Minimize intake of added sugars, as they can cause rapid spikes in blood sugar levels. Look for foods with low or no added sugars.

6. Protein

- **Definition:** Protein is a macronutrient essential for building and repairing tissues, and it also helps maintain muscle mass.
- **Importance:** Include adequate protein in your diet to help with blood sugar control and to promote satiety.

7. Fats

- **Total Fat:** Includes all types of fat in the food.
- **Saturated Fat:** This type of fat is associated with an increased risk of heart disease.
- **Trans Fat:** Artificial trans fats are harmful and should be avoided.
- **Importance:** Choose foods with lower saturated and trans fats. Opt for products that contain healthy fats, such as unsaturated fats found in nuts, seeds, and fish.

8. Sodium

- **Definition:** Sodium is a mineral that is essential for body function but should be consumed in moderation.
- **Importance:** High sodium intake can raise blood pressure and increase the risk of heart disease. Look for foods with lower sodium content.

Practical Tips for Reading Food Labels

1. **Start with the Serving Size:** Always check the serving size first, as all the nutritional information is based on this amount.
2. **Check the Total Carbohydrates:** Focus on the total carbohydrates per serving to manage your carb intake effectively.
3. **Look for Fiber:** Choose foods with higher fiber content to help control blood sugar levels and promote digestive health.
4. **Limit Sugars:** Aim for products with low added sugars to avoid blood sugar spikes.
5. **Monitor Fats:** Opt for foods with lower saturated and trans fats. Prefer products with healthy fats.
6. **Watch Sodium Levels:** Select products with lower sodium content to manage blood pressure.
7. **Review the Ingredient List:** Choose products with whole, natural ingredients and minimal processing.

Identifying Hidden Sugars and Carbs

For individuals managing diabetes, keeping track of sugar and carbohydrate intake is crucial for maintaining stable blood sugar levels. However, hidden sugars and carbohydrates can be found in many processed and packaged foods, making it challenging to manage your diet effectively. Here's how to identify and avoid these hidden sugars and carbs:

1. Reading Ingredient Lists

- **Identify Added Sugars:** Added sugars can appear under many different names. Common names include:
    - Sucrose
    - High fructose corn syrup
    - Corn syrup
    - Dextrose
    - Fructose
    - Glucose
    - Maltose
    - Molasses
    - Cane sugar
    - Agave nectar
    - Honey
    - Maple syrup
- **Order of Ingredients:** Ingredients are listed by weight, from most to least. If any form of sugar appears near the top of the list, the product likely contains a high amount of added sugars.

2. Understanding Nutrition Labels

- **Total Carbohydrates:** This includes all carbs in the food, encompassing dietary fiber, sugars, and starches. Check the total carbohydrates per serving to understand the full impact on your blood sugar.
- **Sugars:** This line includes both naturally occurring sugars and added sugars. The presence of added sugars can be identified by looking at the ingredient list.
- **Added Sugars:** Some labels now list added sugars separately. This information helps you distinguish between natural sugars (like those in fruit) and sugars added during processing.

3. Common Sources of Hidden Sugars and Carbs

- **Condiments and Sauces:** Many condiments like ketchup, barbecue sauce, and salad dressings contain added sugars. Opt for low-sugar or sugar-free versions.
- **Beverages:** Sugary drinks, including soda, fruit juices, flavored waters, and sports drinks, are high in added sugars. Choose water, unsweetened tea, or beverages sweetened with natural alternatives like stevia.
- **Yogurt:** Flavored yogurts often contain significant amounts of added sugars. Choose plain, unsweetened yogurt and add fresh fruit if needed.
- **Snack Foods:** Granola bars, protein bars, and flavored nuts can contain hidden sugars and carbs. Look for products labeled low-carb or sugar-free.
- **Processed Foods:** Packaged and processed foods like breakfast cereals, baked goods, and canned soups often have added sugars. Read labels carefully and choose whole, unprocessed foods whenever possible.
- **Bread and Baked Goods:** Many breads, pastries, and baked goods contain added sugars. Choose whole-grain options and check labels for sugar content.

4. Natural vs. Added Sugars

- **Natural Sugars:** Found in whole foods like fruits, vegetables, and dairy products. These sugars come with fiber, vitamins, and minerals that help mitigate their impact on blood sugar.
- **Added Sugars:** Added during processing or preparation. They offer no nutritional benefits and can cause rapid spikes in blood sugar. Limit foods with high added sugar content.

5. Tips for Reducing Hidden Sugars and Carbs

- **Cook at Home:** Preparing meals at home allows you to control the ingredients and avoid hidden sugars and carbs found in processed foods.
- **Choose Whole Foods:** Focus on whole, unprocessed foods like fruits, vegetables, lean proteins, and whole grains. These foods are less likely to contain hidden sugars and carbs.

- **Use Natural Sweeteners:** When cooking or baking, use natural sweeteners like stevia, erythritol, or monk fruit instead of sugar.
- **Be Skeptical of "Healthy" Labels:** Products labeled "low-fat," "fat-free," or "gluten-free" can still be high in sugars and carbs. Always check the ingredient list and nutrition label.

Identifying hidden sugars and carbs is essential for managing diabetes effectively. By reading ingredient lists, understanding nutrition labels, and being aware of common sources of hidden sugars and carbs, you can make informed dietary choices that support stable blood sugar levels and overall health. Emphasize whole, unprocessed foods and be mindful of the sugar and carbohydrate content in the foods you eat to better manage your diabetes and improve your quality of life.

Meal Planning and Preparation

Creating a Meal Plan

Creating a well-balanced meal plan is crucial for managing diabetes and ensuring you get the right nutrients in the right amounts. Here are some steps and tips to help you create an effective weekly meal plan:

Steps to Create a Weekly Meal Plan:

- **Assess Your Needs:** Determine your daily caloric and nutritional needs based on your health goals, activity level, and dietary requirements. Consult with a healthcare provider or dietitian if needed.
- **Set a Schedule:** Decide how many meals and snacks you will have each day. Consistency in meal timing helps maintain stable blood sugar levels.
- **Choose Recipes:** Select a variety of recipes that include lean proteins, whole grains, healthy fats, and plenty of fruits and vegetables. Aim for a balance of flavors and textures to keep meals interesting.
- **Plan Each Meal:** For each day of the week, plan out your breakfast, lunch, dinner, and snacks. Ensure each meal is balanced and meets your nutritional needs.
- **Make a Shopping List:** Based on your meal plan, create a detailed shopping list of all the ingredients you will need. Check your pantry and fridge to avoid buying items you already have.
- **Prep in Advance:** Prepare as much as you can in advance, such as chopping vegetables, marinating proteins, or cooking grains. This will save time during the week and make it easier to stick to your plan.

Tips for Balancing Different Food Groups:

- **Protein:** Include lean sources such as chicken, turkey, fish, tofu, beans, and legumes. Aim for a serving size of about 3-4 ounces per meal.
- **Carbohydrates:** Choose complex carbohydrates that have a lower glycemic index to help manage blood sugar levels. Options include whole grains like brown rice, quinoa, whole wheat pasta, and starchy vegetables like sweet potatoes.
- **Fruits and Vegetables:** Fill half of your plate with a variety of colorful fruits and vegetables. These provide essential vitamins, minerals, and fiber. Non-starchy vegetables like leafy greens, broccoli, and peppers are particularly beneficial.
- **Healthy Fats:** Incorporate healthy fats from sources like avocados, nuts, seeds, and olive oil. These fats are important for heart health and can help improve satiety.
- **Dairy or Dairy Alternatives:** Choose low-fat or fat-free dairy products or fortified dairy alternatives like almond milk or soy yogurt to ensure adequate calcium and vitamin D intake.
-

Grocery Shopping Tips

Shopping for diabetic-friendly foods requires careful planning and attention to detail. Here are some tips and a suggested grocery list to help you shop effectively:

How to Shop for Diabetic-Friendly Foods:

- **Read Labels:** Always read the nutrition labels to check for added sugars, unhealthy fats, and high sodium levels. Look for foods with high fiber content and low added sugars.

- **Shop the Perimeter:** Most whole foods are found around the perimeter of the grocery store, including fresh produce, lean proteins, and dairy products. Focus your shopping in these areas.
- **Choose Whole Foods:** Opt for whole, unprocessed foods whenever possible. These are less likely to contain hidden sugars and unhealthy additives.
- **Plan Ahead:** Use your meal plan to create a shopping list and stick to it to avoid impulse purchases of unhealthy foods.
- **Buy in Bulk:** Purchase staple items like whole grains, legumes, and nuts in bulk to save money and ensure you always have healthy options on hand.

Suggested Grocery List:

- **Vegetables:** Leafy greens, broccoli, cauliflower, bell peppers, carrots, tomatoes, cucumbers, zucchini, mushrooms.
- **Fruits:** Berries, apples, oranges, pears, peaches, avocados.
- **Proteins:** Chicken breast, turkey, fish, tofu, beans, lentils, eggs, low-fat yogurt, cottage cheese.
- **Whole Grains:** Brown rice, quinoa, whole wheat bread, whole grain pasta, oats.
- **Healthy Fats:** Olive oil, avocado oil, nuts (almonds, walnuts), seeds (chia, flax).
- **Dairy or Alternatives:** Low-fat milk, almond milk, soy yogurt, cheese.
- **Others:** Herbs and spices, garlic, onions, low-sodium broth, canned tomatoes (no added sugar).

Kitchen Essentials

Having the right tools and equipment in your kitchen makes healthy cooking easier and more efficient. Here are some essentials:

Tools and Equipment for Healthy Cooking:

- **Cutting Boards:** Separate boards for meat and vegetables to avoid cross-contamination.
- **Sharp Knives:** Essential for efficient and safe food preparation.
- **Measuring Cups and Spoons:** For accurate portion control and recipe preparation.
- **Non-Stick Cookware:** Reduces the need for added fats when cooking.
- **Blender or Food Processor:** Useful for making smoothies, soups, and sauces.
- **Steamer Basket:** For steaming vegetables to retain nutrients.
- **Slow Cooker or Instant Pot:** For easy, hands-off cooking of healthy meals.
- **Kitchen Scale:** Helps with portion control and accurate measurement of ingredients.

Basic Cooking Techniques for Diabetic Recipes:

- **Grilling:** A healthy way to cook meats and vegetables with minimal added fat.
- **Steaming:** Preserves nutrients in vegetables and is a low-fat cooking method.
- **Baking/Roasting:** Use these methods for meats, fish, and vegetables to enhance flavor without added fats.
- **Sautéing:** Use a small amount of healthy oil (like olive oil) to cook vegetables and lean proteins.
- **Boiling:** Useful for cooking grains and pasta; be sure to measure portions accurately.

By incorporating these meal planning, shopping, and cooking tips, you can create a diabetic-friendly kitchen environment that supports your health goals and makes managing diabetes easier and more enjoyable.

Balanced Breakfasts for Diabetics

1. Veggie Omelet

Yield: 4 servings | Prep time: 15 minutes | Cook time: 10 minutes

Ingredients:

- 8 large eggs
- 1/4 cup milk
- 1/2 teaspoon salt
- 1/4 teaspoon black pepper
- 1 tablespoon olive oil
- 1/2 cup diced bell pepper
- 1/2 cup diced tomatoes
- 1/2 cup chopped spinach
- 1/4 cup diced onions
- 1/4 cup shredded cheddar cheese

Directions:

1. In a medium bowl, whisk together the eggs, milk, salt, and black pepper until well combined.
2. Heat the olive oil in a large skillet over medium heat. Add the bell pepper, tomatoes, spinach, and onions. Sauté for 3-4 minutes until the vegetables are tender.
3. Pour the egg mixture into the skillet, spreading it evenly over the vegetables. Cook for 2-3 minutes until the eggs begin to set around the edges.
4. Sprinkle the shredded cheddar cheese on top. Fold the omelet in half and cook for another 1-2 minutes until the cheese is melted and the eggs are fully cooked. Serve hot.

Nutritional Information: 230 calories, 16g protein, 6g carbohydrates, 15g fat, 2g fiber, 380mg cholesterol, 420mg sodium, 320mg potassium.

2. Whole Grain English Muffin with Peanut Butter

Yield: 2 servings | Prep time: 2 minutes | Cook time: 3 minutes

Ingredients:

- 2 whole grain English muffins
- 4 tablespoons natural peanut butter

Directions:

1. Toast the English muffins until golden brown.
2. Spread 2 tablespoons of peanut butter on each half. Serve warm.

Nutritional Information: 250 calories, 10g protein, 28g carbohydrates, 12g fat, 5g fiber, 0mg cholesterol, 250mg sodium, 300mg potassium.

3. Berry Smoothie Bowl

Yield: 2 servings | Prep time: 5 minutes | Cook time: 0 minutes

Ingredients:

- 1 cup frozen mixed berries
- 1 banana
- 1/2 cup unsweetened almond milk
- 1/4 cup Greek yogurt
- 1 tablespoon chia seeds
- Fresh berries and granola for topping (optional)

Directions:

1. Blend the frozen mixed berries, banana, almond milk, Greek yogurt, and chia seeds until smooth.
2. Pour into bowls and top with fresh berries and granola if desired. Serve immediately.

Nutritional Information: 210 calories, 8g protein, 38g carbohydrates, 5g fat, 8g fiber, 5mg cholesterol, 70mg sodium, 450mg potassium.

4. Greek Yogurt Parfait with Berries

Yield: 4 servings | Prep time: 10 minutes | Cook time: 0 minutes

Ingredients:

- 2 cups plain Greek yogurt
- 1 cup mixed berries (strawberries, blueberries, raspberries)
- 1/2 cup granola
- 2 tablespoons honey
- 1/2 teaspoon vanilla extract

Directions:

1. In a medium bowl, mix the Greek yogurt with the vanilla extract until well combined.
2. In four serving glasses, layer the ingredients starting with 1/4 cup of the yogurt mixture.
3. Add a layer of mixed berries and then a tablespoon of granola.
4. Repeat the layers, finishing with a drizzle of honey on top. Serve immediately.

Nutritional Information: 210 calories, 10g protein, 30g carbohydrates, 6g fat, 3g fiber, 10mg cholesterol, 65mg sodium, 250mg potassium.

5. Avocado Toast on Whole Grain Bread

Yield: 4 servings | Prep time: 10 minutes | Cook time: 5 minutes

Ingredients:

- 4 slices whole grain bread
- 2 ripe avocados
- 1 tablespoon lemon juice
- 1/2 teaspoon salt
- 1/4 teaspoon black pepper
- 1/4 teaspoon red pepper flakes (optional)
- 2 tablespoons chopped fresh cilantro (optional)

Directions:

1. Toast the slices of whole grain bread until golden brown and crisp, about 3-5 minutes.
2. While the bread is toasting, cut the avocados in half, remove the pits, and scoop the flesh into a bowl.
3. Add the lemon juice, salt, and black pepper to the avocado. Mash with a fork until smooth and creamy.
4. Spread the mashed avocado evenly onto the toasted bread slices. Sprinkle with red pepper flakes and cilantro if desired. Serve immediately.

Nutritional Information: 250 calories, 5g protein, 32g carbohydrates, 12g fat, 8g fiber, 0mg cholesterol, 220mg sodium, 450mg potassium.

6. Almond Butter and Apple Slices

Yield: 2 servings | Prep time: 5 minutes | Cook time: 0 minutes

Ingredients:

- 2 medium apples, sliced
- 4 tablespoons almond butter

Directions:

1. Arrange the apple slices on a plate.
2. Serve with almond butter for dipping. Enjoy immediately.

Nutritional Information: 200 calories, 4g protein, 28g carbohydrates, 9g fat, 5g fiber, 0mg cholesterol, 0mg sodium, 250mg potassium.

7. Spinach and Feta Scramble

Yield: 4 servings | Prep time: 5 minutes | Cook time: 10 minutes

Ingredients:

- 8 large eggs
- 1/4 cup milk
- 1 tablespoon olive oil
- 1 cup fresh spinach, chopped
- 1/2 cup feta cheese, crumbled
- 1/4 teaspoon salt
- 1/4 teaspoon black pepper
- 1/4 teaspoon garlic powder (optional)

Directions:

1. In a medium bowl, whisk together the eggs, milk, salt, black pepper, and garlic powder (if using) until well combined.
2. Heat the olive oil in a large skillet over medium heat. Add the chopped spinach and sauté for 2-3 minutes until wilted.
3. Pour the egg mixture into the skillet, stirring gently to combine with the spinach. Cook for 3-5 minutes, stirring occasionally, until the eggs are just set.
4. Sprinkle the crumbled feta cheese over the eggs and cook for an additional 1-2 minutes until the cheese is slightly melted. Serve hot.

Nutritional Information: 210 calories, 14g protein, 3g carbohydrates, 16g fat, 1g fiber, 385mg cholesterol, 440mg sodium, 300mg potassium.

8. Chia Seed Pudding with Almond Milk

Yield: 4 servings | Prep time: 5 minutes | Cook time: 0 minutes (plus 4 hours chilling time)

Ingredients:

- 2 cups unsweetened almond milk
- 1/2 cup chia seeds
- 1 teaspoon vanilla extract
- 2 tablespoons maple syrup or honey (optional)
- Fresh berries or fruit for topping (optional)

Directions:

1. In a medium bowl, whisk together the almond milk, chia seeds, vanilla extract, and maple syrup or honey (if using) until well combined.
2. Let the mixture sit for about 5 minutes, then whisk again to ensure the chia seeds are evenly distributed.
3. Cover the bowl and refrigerate for at least 4 hours, or overnight, until the pudding has thickened.
4. Stir the pudding before serving. Divide into 4 servings and top with fresh berries or fruit if desired.

Nutritional Information: 140 calories, 4g protein, 15g carbohydrates, 7g fat, 10g fiber, 0mg cholesterol, 100mg sodium, 150mg potassium.

9. Oatmeal with Flax Seeds and Fresh Berries

Yield: 4 servings | Prep time: 5 minutes | Cook time: 10 minutes

Ingredients:

- 2 cups old-fashioned rolled oats
- 4 cups water or unsweetened almond milk
- 1/4 cup ground flax seeds
- 1/2 teaspoon cinnamon (optional)
- 1 cup fresh berries (strawberries, blueberries, raspberries)
- 2 tablespoons honey or maple syrup (optional)
- 1/4 teaspoon salt

Directions:

1. In a medium saucepan, bring the water or almond milk to a boil. Add the rolled oats and salt.
2. Reduce heat to medium and cook for 5-7 minutes, stirring occasionally, until the oats are tender and the mixture has thickened.
3. Stir in the ground flax seeds and cinnamon (if using). Cook for an additional 1-2 minutes.
4. Divide the oatmeal into 4 bowls. Top each with fresh berries and drizzle with honey or maple syrup if desired. Serve warm.

Nutritional Information: 220 calories, 7g protein, 40g carbohydrates, 6g fat, 8g fiber, 0mg cholesterol, 80mg sodium, 250mg potassium.

10.   Egg Muffins with Vegetables

Yield: 6 servings | Prep time: 10 minutes | Cook time: 20 minutes

Ingredients:

- 8 large eggs
- 1/2 cup diced bell peppers
- 1/2 cup chopped spinach
- 1/4 cup diced onions
- 1/4 cup shredded cheddar cheese
- 1/4 teaspoon salt
- 1/4 teaspoon black pepper
- 1/4 teaspoon garlic powder (optional)

Directions:

1. Preheat oven to 350°F (175°C). Grease a muffin tin with cooking spray.
2. In a large bowl, whisk together the eggs, salt, black pepper, and garlic powder (if using).
3. Stir in the bell peppers, spinach, onions, and shredded cheddar cheese.
4. Pour the egg mixture evenly into the muffin tin cups.
5. Bake for 18-20 minutes, or until the eggs are set and the tops are golden. Serve warm.

Nutritional Information: 130 calories, 10g protein, 3g carbohydrates, 9g fat, 1g fiber, 220mg cholesterol, 250mg sodium, 150mg potassium.

11.   Low-Carb Breakfast Burrito

Yield: 2 servings | Prep time: 10 minutes | Cook time: 10 minutes

Ingredients:

- 4 large eggs
- 1/4 cup shredded cheddar cheese
- 1/4 cup diced bell peppers
- 1/4 cup diced onions
- 1/4 cup chopped spinach
- 2 low-carb tortillas
- 1 tablespoon olive oil
- 1/4 teaspoon salt
- 1/4 teaspoon black pepper
- Salsa for serving (optional)

Directions:

1. In a medium bowl, whisk together the eggs, salt, and black pepper.
2. Heat the olive oil in a non-stick skillet over medium heat. Add the bell peppers, onions, and spinach. Sauté for 3-4 minutes until tender.
3. Pour the egg mixture into the skillet. Cook, stirring gently, until the eggs are just set. Stir in the shredded cheddar cheese.
4. Divide the egg mixture between the two tortillas. Roll up the tortillas to form burritos. Serve with salsa if desired.

Nutritional Information: 300 calories, 18g protein, 12g carbohydrates, 20g fat, 4g fiber, 380mg cholesterol, 550mg sodium, 400mg potassium.

12.   Smoothie with Spinach, Banana, and Almond Milk

Yield: 2 servings | Prep time: 5 minutes | Cook time: 0 minutes

Ingredients:

- 2 cups unsweetened almond milk
- 2 cups fresh spinach
- 1 banana
- 1 tablespoon chia seeds
- 1/2 teaspoon vanilla extract (optional)

Directions:

1. Add the almond milk, spinach, banana, chia seeds, and vanilla extract (if using) to a blender.
2. Blend until smooth and creamy. Serve immediately.

Nutritional Information: 140 calories, 4g protein, 25g carbohydrates, 3g fat, 6g fiber, 0mg cholesterol, 150mg sodium, 600mg potassium.

13.   Mushroom and Swiss Cheese Omelet

Yield: 2 servings | Prep time: 5 minutes | Cook time: 10 minutes

Ingredients:

- 4 large eggs
- 1/4 cup milk
- 1 cup sliced mushrooms
- 1/2 cup shredded Swiss cheese
- 1 tablespoon butter
- 1/4 teaspoon salt
- 1/4 teaspoon black pepper

Directions:

1. In a medium bowl, whisk together the eggs, milk, salt, and black pepper until well combined.
2. Melt the butter in a non-stick skillet over medium heat. Add the mushrooms and sauté for 3-4 minutes until tender.
3. Pour the egg mixture into the skillet. Cook for 2-3 minutes until the eggs begin to set around the edges.
4. Sprinkle the Swiss cheese over the eggs. Fold the omelet in half and cook for another 1-2 minutes until the cheese is melted and the eggs are fully cooked. Serve hot.

Nutritional Information: 290 calories, 20g protein, 5g carbohydrates, 22g fat, 1g fiber, 400mg cholesterol, 450mg sodium, 300mg potassium.

14.   Low-Carb Pancakes with Almond Flour

Yield: 4 servings | Prep time: 10 minutes | Cook time: 10 minutes

Ingredients:

- 1 cup almond flour
- 1/4 cup unsweetened almond milk
- 2 large eggs
- 1 tablespoon coconut oil, melted
- 1 teaspoon baking powder
- 1/2 teaspoon vanilla extract
- 1/4 teaspoon salt

Directions:

1. In a medium bowl, whisk together the almond flour, baking powder, and salt.
2. In another bowl, mix the almond milk, eggs, melted coconut oil, and vanilla extract.
3. Combine the wet and dry ingredients, stirring until smooth.
4. Heat a non-stick skillet over medium heat and grease lightly with coconut oil. Pour 1/4 cup of batter for each pancake. Cook for 2-3 minutes on each side or until golden brown. Serve warm.

Nutritional Information: 180 calories, 7g protein, 5g carbohydrates, 15g fat, 3g fiber, 45mg cholesterol, 220mg sodium, 150mg potassium.

15.   Scrambled Eggs with Smoked Salmon

Yield: 2 servings | Prep time: 5 minutes | Cook time: 5 minutes

Ingredients:

- 4 large eggs
- 1/4 cup milk
- 2 ounces smoked salmon, chopped
- 1 tablespoon butter
- 1/4 teaspoon salt
- 1/4 teaspoon black pepper
- 1 tablespoon chopped fresh chives (optional)

Directions:

1. In a medium bowl, whisk together the eggs, milk, salt, and black pepper until well combined.
2. Melt the butter in a non-stick skillet over medium heat. Add the egg mixture and cook, stirring gently, until the eggs are just set.
3. Stir in the smoked salmon and cook for an additional 1-2 minutes until warmed through. Sprinkle with chives if desired. Serve immediately.

Nutritional Information: 220 calories, 18g protein, 3g carbohydrates, 15g fat, 0g fiber, 400mg cholesterol, 580mg sodium, 200mg potassium.

16.   Zucchini and Tomato Frittata

Yield: 4 servings | Prep time: 10 minutes | Cook time: 20 minutes

Ingredients:

- 6 large eggs
- 1/4 cup milk
- 1 cup sliced zucchini
- 1/2 cup diced tomatoes
- 1/4 cup grated Parmesan cheese
- 1 tablespoon olive oil
- 1/4 teaspoon salt
- 1/4 teaspoon black pepper

Directions:

1. Preheat the oven to 375°F (190°C).
2. In a medium bowl, whisk together the eggs, milk, salt, and black pepper.
3. Heat the olive oil in an oven-safe skillet over medium heat. Add the zucchini and tomatoes, and cook for 3-4 minutes until tender.
4. Pour the egg mixture into the skillet, spreading it evenly over the vegetables. Cook for 2-3 minutes until the edges begin to set.
5. Sprinkle the grated Parmesan cheese on top. Transfer the skillet to the oven and bake for 15-20 minutes until the eggs are fully set and the top is golden. Serve warm.
6. Nutritional Information: 180 calories, 12g protein, 5g carbohydrates, 13g fat, 1g fiber, 300mg cholesterol, 360mg sodium, 350mg potassium.

17.   Green Smoothie with Kale and Avocado

Yield: 2 servings | Prep time: 5 minutes | Cook time: 0 minutes

Ingredients:

- 2 cups unsweetened almond milk
- 1 cup fresh kale, chopped
- 1/2 avocado
- 1 banana
- 1 tablespoon chia seeds
- 1/2 teaspoon vanilla extract (optional)

Directions:

Add the almond milk, kale, avocado, banana, chia seeds, and vanilla extract (if using) to a blender.

Blend until smooth and creamy. Serve immediately.

Nutritional Information: 180 calories, 5g protein, 23g carbohydrates, 9g fat, 8g fiber, 0mg cholesterol, 90mg sodium, 700mg potassium.

18.   Baked Avocado with Egg

Yield: 2 servings | Prep time: 5 minutes | Cook time: 15 minutes

Ingredients:

- 1 large avocado
- 2 large eggs
- 1/4 teaspoon salt
- 1/4 teaspoon black pepper
- 1 tablespoon chopped fresh chives (optional)

Directions:

1. Preheat the oven to 425°F (220°C). Cut the avocado in half and remove the pit.
2. Scoop out a little of the avocado flesh to make room for the egg. Place the avocado halves in a baking dish.
3. Crack an egg into each avocado half. Season with salt and black pepper.
4. Bake for 12-15 minutes, or until the egg whites are set. Sprinkle with fresh chives if desired. Serve warm.

Nutritional Information: 250 calories, 9g protein, 12g carbohydrates, 20g fat, 7g fiber, 370mg cholesterol, 220mg sodium, 700mg potassium.

19.   Turkey Bacon and Egg Breakfast Sandwich

Yield: 2 servings | Prep time: 5 minutes | Cook time: 10 minutes

Ingredients:

- 4 slices whole grain bread
- 4 slices turkey bacon
- 4 large eggs
- 1 tablespoon olive oil
- 1/4 teaspoon salt
- 1/4 teaspoon black pepper
- 1/2 avocado, sliced (optional)

Directions:

1. Cook the turkey bacon in a skillet over medium heat until crispy. Remove and set aside.
2. In the same skillet, heat the olive oil. Crack the eggs into the skillet, season with salt and black pepper, and cook to your desired doneness.
3. Toast the bread slices. Assemble the sandwiches by placing the eggs and turkey bacon on two slices of bread. Add avocado slices if desired. Top with the remaining bread slices. Serve immediately.

Nutritional Information: 350 calories, 20g protein, 25g carbohydrates, 18g fat, 5g fiber, 410mg cholesterol, 600mg sodium, 400mg potassium.

20.   Quinoa Breakfast Bowl with Berries

Yield: 2 servings | Prep time: 5 minutes | Cook time: 15 minutes

Ingredients:

- 1/2 cup quinoa
- 1 cup water
- 1/2 cup fresh berries (strawberries, blueberries, raspberries)
- 1 tablespoon chia seeds
- 1 tablespoon honey or maple syrup (optional)
- 1/2 teaspoon cinnamon (optional)

Directions:

1. Rinse the quinoa under cold water. In a medium saucepan, bring the quinoa and water to a boil.
2. Reduce the heat to low, cover, and simmer for 15 minutes or until the water is absorbed and the quinoa is tender.
3. Divide the quinoa between two bowls. Top with fresh berries, chia seeds, honey or maple syrup (if using), and a sprinkle of cinnamon. Serve warm.

Nutritional Information: 220 calories, 7g protein, 40g carbohydrates, 5g fat, 8g fiber, 0mg cholesterol, 10mg sodium, 400mg potassium.

21.   Ricotta Cheese with Fresh Raspberries

Yield: 2 servings | Prep time: 5 minutes | Cook time: 0 minutes

Ingredients:

- 1 cup ricotta cheese
- 1/2 cup fresh raspberries
- 1 tablespoon honey or maple syrup (optional)

Directions:

1. Divide the ricotta cheese between two bowls.
2. Top each with fresh raspberries and drizzle with honey or maple syrup if desired. Serve immediately.

Nutritional Information: 160 calories, 8g protein, 15g carbohydrates, 8g fat, 2g fiber, 30mg cholesterol, 50mg sodium, 150mg potassium.

22.   Pumpkin Spice Chia Pudding

Yield: 2 servings | Prep time: 5 minutes | Cook time: 0 minutes (plus 4 hours chilling time)

Ingredients:

- 2 cups unsweetened almond milk
- 1/2 cup chia seeds
- 1/2 cup pumpkin puree
- 1 teaspoon vanilla extract
- 1 teaspoon pumpkin pie spice
- 2 tablespoons maple syrup or honey (optional)

Directions:

1. In a medium bowl, whisk together the almond milk, chia seeds, pumpkin puree, vanilla extract, pumpkin pie spice, and maple syrup or honey (if using) until well combined.
2. Let the mixture sit for about 5 minutes, then whisk again to ensure the chia seeds are evenly distributed.
3. Cover the bowl and refrigerate for at least 4 hours, or overnight, until the pudding has thickened.
4. Stir the pudding before serving. Divide into two servings and enjoy.

Nutritional Information: 180 calories, 5g protein, 24g carbohydrates, 9g fat, 11g fiber, 0mg cholesterol, 90mg sodium, 300mg potassium.

23.   Protein Pancakes with Greek Yogurt

Yield: 4 servings | Prep time: 10 minutes | Cook time: 10 minutes

Ingredients:

- 1 cup Greek yogurt
- 1/2 cup rolled oats
- 1/2 cup cottage cheese
- 2 large eggs
- 1 teaspoon baking powder
- 1/2 teaspoon vanilla extract
- 1/4 teaspoon salt

Directions:

1. Blend all the ingredients in a blender until smooth.
2. Heat a non-stick skillet over medium heat and grease lightly with cooking spray or a little oil.
3. Pour 1/4 cup of batter for each pancake. Cook for 2-3 minutes on each side or until golden brown. Serve warm.

Nutritional Information: 200 calories, 15g protein, 20g carbohydrates, 7g fat, 2g fiber, 120mg cholesterol, 250mg sodium, 200mg potassium.

24.   Low-Carb Bagel with Cream Cheese and Cucumber

Yield: 2 servings | Prep time: 5 minutes | Cook time: 10 minutes

Ingredients:

- 2 low-carb bagels
- 4 tablespoons cream cheese
- 1/2 cucumber, thinly sliced
- 1/4 teaspoon salt
- 1/4 teaspoon black pepper

Directions:

1. Toast the bagels until golden brown.
2. Spread 2 tablespoons of cream cheese on each bagel half.
3. Top with cucumber slices and season with salt and black pepper. Serve immediately.

Nutritional Information: 220 calories, 8g protein, 15g carbohydrates, 14g fat, 3g fiber, 40mg cholesterol, 360mg sodium, 250mg potassium.

25.   Berry and Spinach Smoothie

Yield: 2 servings | Prep time: 5 minutes | Cook time: 0 minutes

Ingredients:

- 1 cup unsweetened almond milk
- 1 cup fresh spinach
- 1 cup frozen mixed berries
- 1 banana
- 1 tablespoon chia seeds

Directions:

1. Add the almond milk, spinach, mixed berries, banana, and chia seeds to a blender.
2. Blend until smooth and creamy. Serve immediately.

Nutritional Information: 160 calories, 4g protein, 35g carbohydrates, 3g fat, 8g fiber, 0mg cholesterol, 100mg sodium, 600mg potassium.

26.   Cauliflower Hash Browns

Yield: 4 servings | Prep time: 10 minutes | Cook time: 20 minutes

Ingredients:

- 4 cups grated cauliflower
- 1/2 cup shredded cheddar cheese
- 1/4 cup almond flour
- 2 large eggs
- 1/4 teaspoon garlic powder
- 1/4 teaspoon salt
- 1/4 teaspoon black pepper
- 1 tablespoon olive oil

Directions:

1. Preheat the oven to 400°F (200°C) and line a baking sheet with parchment paper.
2. In a large bowl, combine the grated cauliflower, cheddar cheese, almond flour, eggs, garlic powder, salt, and black pepper. Mix until well combined.
3. Scoop 1/4 cup of the mixture and shape into hash brown patties. Place on the prepared baking sheet.
4. Drizzle with olive oil and bake for 15-20 minutes, or until golden brown and crispy. Serve warm.

Nutritional Information: 150 calories, 8g protein, 6g carbohydrates, 10g fat, 3g fiber, 70mg cholesterol, 300mg sodium, 350mg potassium.

27.   Mango and Coconut Chia Pudding

Yield: 2 servings | Prep time: 5 minutes | Cook time: 0 minutes (plus 4 hours chilling time)

Ingredients:

- 2 cups unsweetened coconut milk
- 1/2 cup chia seeds
- 1/2 cup mango puree
- 1 teaspoon vanilla extract
- 1 tablespoon maple syrup or honey (optional)

Directions:

1. In a medium bowl, whisk together the coconut milk, chia seeds, mango puree, vanilla extract, and maple syrup or honey (if using) until well combined.
2. Let the mixture sit for about 5 minutes, then whisk again to ensure the chia seeds are evenly distributed.
3. Cover the bowl and refrigerate for at least 4 hours, or overnight, until the pudding has thickened.
4. Stir the pudding before serving. Divide into two servings and enjoy.

Nutritional Information: 180 calories, 5g protein, 20g carbohydrates, 9g fat, 11g fiber, 0mg cholesterol, 50mg sodium, 300mg potassium.

28.   Stuffed Bell Peppers with Eggs

Yield: 4 servings | Prep time: 10 minutes | Cook time: 25 minutes

Ingredients:

- 4 large bell peppers
- 8 large eggs
- 1/4 cup diced onions
- 1/4 cup diced tomatoes
- 1/4 cup chopped spinach
- 1/4 cup shredded cheddar cheese
- 1/4 teaspoon salt
- 1/4 teaspoon black pepper

Directions:

1. Preheat the oven to 375°F (190°C). Cut the tops off the bell peppers and remove the seeds.
2. In a medium bowl, whisk together the eggs, onions, tomatoes, spinach, salt, and black pepper until well combined.
3. Place the bell peppers in a baking dish and fill each with the egg mixture.
4. Bake for 20-25 minutes, or until the eggs are set. Sprinkle with shredded cheddar cheese and bake for an additional 5 minutes, or until the cheese is melted. Serve warm.

Nutritional Information: 220 calories, 14g protein, 10g carbohydrates, 14g fat, 3g fiber, 370mg cholesterol, 300mg sodium, 450mg potassium.

29.   Green Tea Smoothie with Matcha

Yield: 2 servings | Prep time: 5 minutes | Cook time: 0 minutes

Ingredients:

- 1 cup unsweetened almond milk
- 1 cup spinach
- 1 banana
- 1 teaspoon matcha green tea powder
- 1 tablespoon chia seeds

Directions:

1. Add the almond milk, spinach, banana, matcha powder, and chia seeds to a blender.
2. Blend until smooth and creamy. Serve immediately.

Nutritional Information: 130 calories, 3g protein, 25g carbohydrates, 3g fat, 6g fiber, 0mg cholesterol, 90mg sodium, 400mg potassium.

30.   Cinnamon and Apple Oatmeal

Yield: 4 servings | Prep time: 5 minutes | Cook time: 10 minutes

Ingredients:

- 2 cups old-fashioned rolled oats
- 4 cups water or unsweetened almond milk
- 1 apple, diced
- 1 teaspoon ground cinnamon
- 1/4 teaspoon salt
- 1 tablespoon maple syrup or honey (optional)

Directions:

1. In a medium saucepan, bring the water or almond milk to a boil. Add the rolled oats, diced apple, ground cinnamon, and salt.
2. Reduce heat to medium and cook for 5-7 minutes, stirring occasionally, until the oats are tender and the mixture has thickened.
3. Stir in the maple syrup or honey (if using). Divide into four bowls and serve warm.

Nutritional Information: 190 calories, 5g protein, 35g carbohydrates, 3g fat, 5g fiber, 0mg cholesterol, 100mg sodium, 200mg potassium.

31.   Spicy Avocado Egg Toast

Yield: 2 servings | Prep time: 5 minutes | Cook time: 5 minutes

Ingredients:

- 2 slices whole grain bread
- 1 ripe avocado
- 2 large eggs
- 1 tablespoon olive oil
- 1/4 teaspoon red pepper flakes
- 1/4 teaspoon salt
- 1/4 teaspoon black pepper

Directions:

1. Toast the bread slices until golden brown.
2. While the bread is toasting, heat the olive oil in a non-stick skillet over medium heat. Crack the eggs into the skillet and cook to your desired doneness.
3. Mash the avocado and spread it evenly onto the toasted bread. Top with the cooked eggs.
4. Sprinkle with red pepper flakes, salt, and black pepper. Serve immediately.

Nutritional Information: 300 calories, 12g protein, 24g carbohydrates, 20g fat, 8g fiber, 370mg cholesterol, 280mg sodium, 500mg potassium.

32.   Vegetable and Cheese Breakfast Quiche

Yield: 6 servings | Prep time: 10 minutes | Cook time: 35 minutes

Ingredients:

- 1 pre-made whole wheat pie crust
- 6 large eggs
- 1/2 cup milk
- 1 cup chopped spinach
- 1/2 cup diced bell peppers
- 1/2 cup diced onions
- 1 cup shredded cheddar cheese
- 1/4 teaspoon salt
- 1/4 teaspoon black pepper

Directions:

1. Preheat the oven to 375°F (190°C). Place the pie crust in a pie dish and set aside.
2. In a large bowl, whisk together the eggs, milk, salt, and black pepper until well combined.
3. Stir in the spinach, bell peppers, onions, and shredded cheddar cheese.
4. Pour the egg mixture into the pie crust. Bake for 30-35 minutes, or until the eggs are set and the top is golden. Serve warm.

Nutritional Information: 300 calories, 14g protein, 20g carbohydrates, 20g fat, 2g fiber, 300mg cholesterol, 400mg sodium, 300mg potassium.

33.   Overnight Oats with Chia Seeds and Almonds

Yield: 4 servings | Prep time: 5 minutes | Cook time: 0 minutes (plus overnight refrigeration)

Ingredients:

- 2 cups old-fashioned rolled oats
- 2 cups unsweetened almond milk
- 1/4 cup chia seeds
- 1/4 cup sliced almonds
- 1 tablespoon maple syrup or honey (optional)
- 1 teaspoon vanilla extract (optional)

Directions:

1. In a large bowl, combine the rolled oats, almond milk, chia seeds, sliced almonds, maple syrup or honey (if using), and vanilla extract (if using). Stir until well mixed.
2. Cover the bowl and refrigerate overnight.
3. Stir the mixture before serving. Divide into four bowls and enjoy.

Nutritional Information: 220 calories, 6g protein, 30g carbohydrates, 8g fat, 8g fiber, 0mg cholesterol, 60mg sodium, 300mg potassium.

34.   Ham and Cheese Breakfast Wrap

Yield: 2 servings | Prep time: 5 minutes | Cook time: 5 minutes

Ingredients:

- 2 whole grain tortillas
- 4 slices deli ham
- 1/2 cup shredded cheddar cheese
- 2 large eggs
- 1 tablespoon olive oil
- 1/4 teaspoon salt
- 1/4 teaspoon black pepper

Directions:

1. Heat the olive oil in a non-stick skillet over medium heat. Crack the eggs into the skillet, season with salt and black pepper, and scramble until fully cooked.
2. Place the tortillas on a flat surface. Divide the scrambled eggs, ham slices, and shredded cheddar cheese between the two tortillas.
3. Roll up the tortillas to form wraps. Serve immediately.

Nutritional Information: 300 calories, 18g protein, 24g carbohydrates, 15g fat, 2g fiber, 380mg cholesterol, 800mg sodium, 350mg potassium.

35. Berry Chia Jam on Whole Grain Toast

Yield: 2 servings | Prep time: 10 minutes | Cook time: 5 minutes

Ingredients:

- 1 cup fresh or frozen mixed berries
- 2 tablespoons chia seeds
- 1 tablespoon honey or maple syrup (optional)
- 4 slices whole grain bread

Directions:

1. In a small saucepan, heat the mixed berries over medium heat until they begin to break down, about 5 minutes.
2. Mash the berries with a fork or potato masher to your desired consistency. Stir in the chia seeds and honey or maple syrup (if using).
3. Remove from heat and let the chia jam cool and thicken.
4. Toast the bread slices. Spread the chia jam evenly onto the toast. Serve immediately.

Nutritional Information: 180 calories, 6g protein, 28g carbohydrates, 5g fat, 8g fiber, 0mg cholesterol, 200mg sodium, 150mg potassium.

36. Egg and Spinach Breakfast Muffins

Yield: 6 servings | Prep time: 10 minutes | Cook time: 20 minutes

Ingredients:

- 8 large eggs
- 1 cup chopped spinach
- 1/2 cup diced bell peppers
- 1/4 cup diced onions
- 1/4 cup shredded cheddar cheese
- 1/4 teaspoon salt
- 1/4 teaspoon black pepper
- 1/4 teaspoon garlic powder (optional)

Directions:

1. Preheat oven to 350°F (175°C). Grease a muffin tin with cooking spray.
2. In a large bowl, whisk together the eggs, salt, black pepper, and garlic powder (if using).
3. Stir in the spinach, bell peppers, onions, and shredded cheddar cheese.
4. Pour the egg mixture evenly into the muffin tin cups.
5. Bake for 18-20 minutes, or until the eggs are set and the tops are golden. Serve warm.

Nutritional Information: 130 calories, 10g protein, 3g carbohydrates, 9g fat, 1g fiber, 220mg cholesterol, 250mg sodium, 150mg potassium.

37.   Tofu Scramble with Veggies

Yield: 4 servings | Prep time: 10 minutes | Cook time: 10 minutes

Ingredients:

- 1 block (14 ounces) firm tofu, drained and crumbled
- 1 tablespoon olive oil
- 1/2 cup diced bell peppers
- 1/2 cup diced tomatoes
- 1/2 cup chopped spinach
- 1/4 cup diced onions
- 1/4 teaspoon turmeric
- 1/4 teaspoon salt
- 1/4 teaspoon black pepper

Directions:

1. Heat the olive oil in a large skillet over medium heat. Add the bell peppers, tomatoes, spinach, and onions. Sauté for 3-4 minutes until tender.
2. Add the crumbled tofu, turmeric, salt, and black pepper to the skillet. Cook for 5-7 minutes, stirring occasionally, until the tofu is heated through and slightly browned. Serve warm.

Nutritional Information: 150 calories, 12g protein, 6g carbohydrates, 10g fat, 2g fiber, 0mg cholesterol, 350mg sodium, 250mg potassium.

38.   Low-Carb Waffles with Berries

Yield: 4 servings | Prep time: 10 minutes | Cook time: 10 minutes

Ingredients:

- 1 cup almond flour
- 1/4 cup unsweetened almond milk
- 2 large eggs
- 1 tablespoon coconut oil, melted
- 1 teaspoon baking powder
- 1/2 teaspoon vanilla extract
- 1/4 teaspoon salt
- 1/2 cup fresh berries for topping

Directions:

1. In a medium bowl, whisk together the almond flour, baking powder, and salt.
2. In another bowl, mix the almond milk, eggs, melted coconut oil, and vanilla extract.
3. Combine the wet and dry ingredients, stirring until smooth.
4. Preheat a waffle iron and grease lightly with cooking spray or a little oil. Pour the batter into the waffle iron and cook according to the manufacturer's instructions. Serve warm with fresh berries.

Nutritional Information: 200 calories, 7g protein, 6g carbohydrates, 16g fat, 3g fiber, 45mg cholesterol, 220mg sodium,150mg potassium.

Wholesome Lunches for Diabetics

39.   Spaghetti Squash with Marinara Sauce

Yield: 4 servings | Prep time: 10 minutes | Cook time: 40 minutes

Ingredients:

- 1 large spaghetti squash
- 2 cups marinara sauce
- 1/4 cup grated Parmesan cheese
- 1 tablespoon olive oil

- 1/4 teaspoon salt
- 1/4 teaspoon black pepper
- 1/4 cup fresh basil leaves, chopped (optional)

Directions:

1. Preheat the oven to 400°F (200°C). Cut the spaghetti squash in half lengthwise and remove the seeds.
2. Drizzle the cut sides with olive oil and season with salt and black pepper. Place the squash halves cut side down on a baking sheet and bake for 35-40 minutes, or until the squash is tender.
3. While the squash is baking, heat the marinara sauce in a saucepan over medium heat.
4. When the squash is done, use a fork to scrape out the flesh into spaghetti-like strands. Divide the strands among four plates and top with marinara sauce and grated Parmesan cheese. Garnish with fresh basil if desired. Serve warm.

Nutritional Information: 200 calories, 6g protein, 30g carbohydrates, 8g fat, 6g fiber, 10mg cholesterol, 600mg sodium, 800mg potassium.

40.   Chickpea Salad with Lemon Dressing

Yield: 4 servings | Prep time: 10 minutes | Cook time: 0 minutes

Ingredients:

- 2 cans (15 oz each) chickpeas, rinsed and drained
- 1 cup cherry tomatoes, halved
- 1/2 cucumber, diced
- 1/4 red onion, thinly sliced
- 1/4 cup fresh parsley, chopped

- 1/4 cup olive oil
- 2 tablespoons lemon juice
- 1 teaspoon lemon zest
- 1/2 teaspoon salt
- 1/4 teaspoon black pepper

Directions:

1. In a large bowl, combine the chickpeas, cherry tomatoes, cucumber, red onion, and fresh parsley.
2. In a small bowl, whisk together the olive oil, lemon juice, lemon zest, salt, and black pepper. Pour over the chickpea mixture and toss to coat. Serve immediately.

Nutritional Information: 250 calories, 8g protein, 30g carbohydrates, 12g fat, 8g fiber, 0mg cholesterol, 600mg sodium, 600mg potassium.

41. Moroccan Lentil Stew

Yield: 6 servings | Prep time: 10 minutes | Cook time: 30 minutes

Ingredients:

- 1 tablespoon olive oil
- 1 onion, diced
- 2 carrots, diced
- 2 celery stalks, diced
- 3 cloves garlic, minced
- 1 cup dried lentils, rinsed
- 1 can (14.5 oz) diced tomatoes
- 4 cups vegetable broth
- 1 teaspoon ground cumin
- 1 teaspoon ground coriander
- 1/2 teaspoon ground cinnamon
- 1/2 teaspoon ground turmeric
- 1/4 teaspoon cayenne pepper (optional)
- 1/4 teaspoon salt
- 1/4 teaspoon black pepper
- 1/4 cup fresh cilantro, chopped (optional)

Directions:

1. Heat the olive oil in a large pot over medium heat. Add the onion, carrots, and celery. Sauté for 5-7 minutes until softened.
2. Add the garlic and cook for another 1-2 minutes until fragrant.
3. Stir in the lentils, diced tomatoes, vegetable broth, ground cumin, ground coriander, ground cinnamon, ground turmeric, cayenne pepper (if using), salt, and black pepper. Bring to a boil, then reduce heat and simmer for 25-30 minutes, or until the lentils are tender.
4. Stir in the fresh cilantro (if using) and serve hot.

Nutritional Information: 250 calories, 12g protein, 38g carbohydrates, 6g fat, 12g fiber, 0mg cholesterol, 600mg sodium, 700mg potassium.

42. Lentil and Cucumber Salad

Yield: 4 servings | Prep time: 10 minutes | Cook time: 20 minutes

Ingredients:

- 1 cup lentils, rinsed
- 2 cups water
- 1 cucumber, diced
- 1/2 red onion, chopped
- 1/4 cup parsley, chopped
- 2 tablespoons olive oil
- 2 tablespoons lemon juice
- 1/2 teaspoon salt
- 1/4 teaspoon black pepper

Directions:

1. In a saucepan, bring lentils and water to a boil. Reduce heat and simmer for 20 minutes, until tender. Drain and cool.
2. In a bowl, combine lentils, cucumber, red onion, and parsley.
3. Whisk together olive oil, lemon juice, salt, and pepper. Pour over salad and toss to coat. Serve chilled.

Nutritional Information: 220 calories, 10g protein, 30g carbohydrates, 8g fat, 10g fiber, 0mg cholesterol, 300mg sodium, 400mg potassium.

43.   Vegetable and Hummus Wrap

Yield: 4 servings | Prep time: 10 minutes | Cook time: 0 minutes

Ingredients:

- 4 whole grain tortillas
- 1 cup hummus
- 1 cup shredded carrots
- 1 cup sliced cucumbers
- 1/2 cup red bell pepper, sliced
- 1/2 cup yellow bell pepper, sliced
- 1 cup fresh spinach leaves
- 1/4 teaspoon salt
- 1/4 teaspoon black pepper

Directions:

1. Lay out the tortillas on a flat surface. Spread 1/4 cup of hummus on each tortilla.
2. Divide the shredded carrots, sliced cucumbers, red bell pepper, yellow bell pepper, and spinach leaves evenly among the tortillas.
3. Season with salt and black pepper.
4. Roll up the tortillas tightly to form wraps. Serve immediately.

Nutritional Information: 250 calories, 8g protein, 40g carbohydrates, 8g fat, 10g fiber, 0mg cholesterol, 600mg sodium, 700mg potassium.

44.   Zucchini Noodles with Pesto and Cherry Tomatoes

Yield: 4 servings | Prep time: 10 minutes | Cook time: 10 minutes

Ingredients:

- 4 medium zucchinis, spiralized into noodles
- 2 cups cherry tomatoes, halved
- 1/4 cup basil pesto (store-bought or homemade)
- 1 tablespoon olive oil
- 2 cloves garlic, minced
- 1/4 cup grated Parmesan cheese (optional)
- 1/4 teaspoon salt
- 1/4 teaspoon black pepper
- Fresh basil leaves for garnish (optional)

Directions:

1. In a large skillet, heat olive oil over medium heat. Add minced garlic and cook until fragrant, about 1 minute.
2. Add the zucchini noodles and cook for 3-4 minutes until tender but still slightly crisp.
3. Stir in the cherry tomatoes and cook for another 2 minutes.
4. Remove from heat and toss with basil pesto until evenly coated.
5. Season with salt and black pepper to taste. Sprinkle with grated Parmesan cheese and garnish with fresh basil leaves, if desired. Serve immediately.

Nutritional Information: 200 calories, 6g protein, 12g carbohydrates, 14g fat, 4g fiber, 5mg cholesterol, 300mg sodium, 500mg potassium.

45.   Spinach and Feta Stuffed Chicken

Yield: 4 servings | Prep time: 15 minutes | Cook time: 25 minutes

Ingredients:

- 4 boneless, skinless chicken breasts
- 1 cup fresh spinach, chopped
- 1/2 cup crumbled feta cheese
- 2 cloves garlic, minced

- 1 tablespoon olive oil
- 1/4 teaspoon salt
- 1/4 teaspoon black pepper
- 1 teaspoon dried oregano

Directions:

1. Preheat the oven to 375°F (190°C).
2. In a bowl, mix spinach, feta cheese, garlic, salt, and pepper.
3. Slice a pocket into each chicken breast and stuff with the spinach mixture.
4. Secure with toothpicks.
5. Heat olive oil in a skillet over medium-high heat. Brown chicken on both sides, about 3 minutes per side.
6. Transfer to a baking dish and sprinkle with dried oregano.
7. Bake for 20-25 minutes or until the chicken is cooked through. Serve immediately.

Nutritional Information: 280 calories, 32g protein, 4g carbohydrates, 15g fat, 2g fiber, 90mg cholesterol, 350mg sodium, 400mg potassium.

46.   Turkey and Spinach Stuffed Mushrooms

Yield: 4 servings | Prep time: 15 minutes | Cook time: 20 minutes

Ingredients:

- 8 large Portobello mushrooms
- 1 pound ground turkey
- 2 cups fresh spinach, chopped
- 1/2 cup ricotta cheese
- 1/4 cup grated Parmesan cheese

- 2 cloves garlic, minced
- 1 tablespoon olive oil
- 1/4 teaspoon salt
- 1/4 teaspoon black pepper

Directions:

1. Preheat the oven to 375°F (190°C).
2. Remove stems from mushrooms and brush caps with olive oil. Place on a baking sheet.
3. In a skillet, cook ground turkey and garlic until browned. Add spinach and cook until wilted.
4. Remove from heat and mix in ricotta cheese, salt, and pepper.
5. Stuff mushroom caps with the turkey mixture and sprinkle with Parmesan cheese.
6. Bake for 15-20 minutes until mushrooms are tender and cheese is golden. Serve hot.

Nutritional Information: 250 calories, 25g protein, 10g carbohydrates, 12g fat, 3g fiber, 70mg cholesterol, 400mg sodium, 500mg potassium.

47.   Quinoa and Veggie Stir-Fry

Yield: 4 servings | Prep time: 10 minutes | Cook time: 15 minutes

Ingredients:

- 1 cup quinoa, rinsed
- 2 cups water
- 1 tablespoon olive oil
- 1 red bell pepper, diced
- 1 cup broccoli florets
- 1 carrot, julienned
- 2 cloves garlic, minced
- 2 tablespoons soy sauce (low-sodium)
- 1 teaspoon sesame oil
- 1/4 teaspoon salt
- 1/4 teaspoon black pepper

Directions:

1. In a saucepan, bring quinoa and water to a boil. Reduce heat, cover, and simmer for 15 minutes or until water is absorbed.
2. In a large skillet, heat olive oil over medium-high heat. Add garlic, bell pepper, broccoli, and carrot. Stir-fry for 5-7 minutes.
3. Add cooked quinoa to the skillet. Stir in soy sauce, sesame oil, salt, and black pepper. Cook for 2-3 minutes.
4. Serve hot.

Nutritional Information: 240 calories, 8g protein, 36g carbohydrates, 8g fat, 5g fiber, 0mg cholesterol, 350mg sodium, 600mg potassium.

48.   Quinoa and Black Bean Bowl

Yield: 4 servings | Prep time: 10 minutes | Cook time: 20 minutes

Ingredients:

- 1 cup quinoa
- 2 cups water
- 1 can (15 oz) black beans, rinsed and drained
- 1 cup corn kernels (fresh or frozen)
- 1 red bell pepper, diced
- 1/4 cup red onion, diced
- 1/4 cup cilantro, chopped
- 2 tablespoons olive oil
- 2 tablespoons lime juice
- 1 teaspoon ground cumin
- 1/2 teaspoon salt
- 1/4 teaspoon black pepper

Directions:

1. Rinse the quinoa under cold water. In a medium saucepan, bring the quinoa and water to a boil.
2. Reduce the heat to low, cover, and simmer for 15 minutes, or until the water is absorbed and the quinoa is tender.
3. In a large bowl, combine the cooked quinoa, black beans, corn, red bell pepper, red onion, and cilantro.
4. In a small bowl, whisk together the olive oil, lime juice, ground cumin, salt, and black pepper. Pour over the quinoa mixture and toss to coat.
5. Serve immediately or refrigerate for later.

Nutritional Information: 280 calories, 10g protein, 45g carbohydrates, 8g fat, 8g fiber, 0mg cholesterol, 300mg sodium, 700mg potassium.

49. Grilled Chicken Salad

Yield: 4 servings | Prep time: 15 minutes | Cook time: 10 minutes

Ingredients:

- 2 boneless, skinless chicken breasts
- 6 cups mixed greens
- 1 cup cherry tomatoes, halved
- 1/2 cucumber, sliced
- 1/4 red onion, thinly sliced
- 1/4 cup feta cheese, crumbled

- 2 tablespoons olive oil
- 2 tablespoons balsamic vinegar
- 1 teaspoon Dijon mustard
- 1/4 teaspoon salt
- 1/4 teaspoon black pepper

Directions:

1. Preheat a grill to medium-high heat. Season the chicken breasts with salt and black pepper.
2. Grill the chicken for 5-7 minutes on each side, or until fully cooked. Let cool and slice.
3. In a large bowl, combine the mixed greens, cherry tomatoes, cucumber, red onion, and feta cheese.
4. In a small bowl, whisk together the olive oil, balsamic vinegar, Dijon mustard, salt, and black pepper. Drizzle over the salad and toss to coat.
5. Top the salad with the sliced grilled chicken. Serve immediately.

Nutritional Information: 300 calories, 30g protein, 10g carbohydrates, 15g fat, 3g fiber, 80mg cholesterol, 400mg sodium, 500mg potassium.

50. Chicken and Cauliflower Rice Bowl

Yield: 4 servings | Prep time: 10 minutes | Cook time: 15 minutes

Ingredients:

- 2 boneless, skinless chicken breasts, diced
- 4 cups cauliflower rice
- 1 cup diced bell peppers
- 1 cup diced zucchini
- 2 cloves garlic, minced

- 2 tablespoons soy sauce (low-sodium)
- 1 tablespoon olive oil
- 1/4 teaspoon salt
- 1/4 teaspoon black pepper

Directions:

1. In a large skillet, heat the olive oil over medium heat. Add the diced chicken, salt, and black pepper. Cook until the chicken is no longer pink, about 5-7 minutes.
2. Add the garlic, bell peppers, and zucchini. Cook for an additional 3-4 minutes until the vegetables are tender.
3. Stir in the cauliflower rice and soy sauce. Cook for another 3-4 minutes until the cauliflower rice is heated through. Serve hot.

Nutritional Information: 300 calories, 25g protein, 15g carbohydrates, 12g fat, 5g fiber, 60mg cholesterol, 600mg sodium, 600mg potassium.

51.   Turkey and Avocado Wrap

Yield: 4 servings | Prep time: 10 minutes | Cook time: 0 minutes

Ingredients:

- 4 whole grain tortillas
- 8 ounces sliced turkey breast
- 1 avocado, sliced
- 1 cup spinach leaves
- 1/2 cup shredded carrots
- 1/4 cup hummus
- 1/4 teaspoon salt
- 1/4 teaspoon black pepper

Directions:

1. Lay out the tortillas on a flat surface. Spread 1 tablespoon of hummus on each tortilla.
2. Divide the turkey, avocado, spinach, and shredded carrots evenly among the tortillas.
3. Season with salt and black pepper.
4. Roll up the tortillas tightly to form wraps. Serve immediately.

Nutritional Information: 320 calories, 20g protein, 30g carbohydrates, 15g fat, 8g fiber, 40mg cholesterol, 500mg sodium, 700mg potassium.

52.   Lentil Soup

Yield: 6 servings | Prep time: 10 minutes | Cook time: 30 minutes

Ingredients:

- 1 cup dried lentils, rinsed
- 6 cups vegetable broth
- 1 onion, diced
- 2 carrots, diced
- 2 celery stalks, diced
- 3 cloves garlic, minced
- 1 can (14.5 oz) diced tomatoes
- 1 teaspoon ground cumin
- 1/2 teaspoon dried thyme
- 1/4 teaspoon salt
- 1/4 teaspoon black pepper
- 2 tablespoons olive oil

Directions:

1. Heat the olive oil in a large pot over medium heat. Add the onion, carrots, and celery. Sauté for 5-7 minutes until softened.
2. Add the garlic, ground cumin, dried thyme, salt, and black pepper. Cook for another 1-2 minutes until fragrant.
3. Add the lentils, vegetable broth, and diced tomatoes. Bring to a boil, then reduce heat and simmer for 25-30 minutes until the lentils are tender.
4. Serve hot, garnished with fresh herbs if desired.

Nutritional Information: 250 calories, 12g protein, 38g carbohydrates, 6g fat, 12g fiber, 0mg cholesterol, 600mg sodium, 700mg potassium.

53. Chicken and Veggie Stir-Fry

Yield: 4 servings | Prep time: 15 minutes | Cook time: 15 minutes

Ingredients:

- 2 boneless, skinless chicken breasts, cut into thin strips
- 2 cups broccoli florets
- 1 red bell pepper, sliced
- 1 yellow bell pepper, sliced
- 1 cup snap peas
- 2 cloves garlic, minced
- 1 tablespoon fresh ginger, grated
- 3 tablespoons soy sauce (low-sodium)
- 2 tablespoons olive oil
- 1 tablespoon cornstarch
- 1/4 teaspoon red pepper flakes (optional)

Directions:

1. In a small bowl, mix the soy sauce and cornstarch until smooth.
2. Heat 1 tablespoon of olive oil in a large skillet or wok over medium-high heat. Add the chicken strips and cook until no longer pink, about 5-7 minutes. Remove from the skillet and set aside.
3. Add the remaining olive oil to the skillet. Add the broccoli, bell peppers, snap peas, garlic, and ginger. Sauté for 5-7 minutes until the vegetables are tender-crisp.
4. Return the chicken to the skillet. Pour the soy sauce mixture over the chicken and vegetables. Cook for another 2-3 minutes, stirring frequently, until the sauce has thickened. Serve hot.

Nutritional Information: 300 calories, 25g protein, 20g carbohydrates, 12g fat, 5g fiber, 60mg cholesterol, 700mg sodium, 600mg potassium.

54. Caprese Salad with Balsamic Glaze

Yield: 4 servings | Prep time: 10 minutes | Cook time: 0 minutes

Ingredients:

- 4 large tomatoes, sliced
- 8 ounces fresh mozzarella, sliced
- 1/4 cup fresh basil leaves
- 2 tablespoons balsamic glaze
- 2 tablespoons olive oil
- 1/4 teaspoon salt
- 1/4 teaspoon black pepper

Directions:

1. Arrange the tomato slices and mozzarella slices on a serving platter, alternating between them.
2. Tuck the basil leaves between the tomato and mozzarella slices.
3. Drizzle with olive oil and balsamic glaze. Season with salt and black pepper. Serve immediately.

Nutritional Information: 250 calories, 12g protein, 10g carbohydrates, 18g fat, 2g fiber, 50mg cholesterol, 350mg sodium, 400mg potassium.

55. Tuna Salad Lettuce Wraps

Yield: 4 servings | Prep time: 10 minutes | Cook time: 0 minutes

Ingredients:

- 2 cans (5 oz each) tuna, drained
- 1/4 cup Greek yogurt
- 1 tablespoon Dijon mustard
- 1 celery stalk, diced
- 1/4 cup red onion, diced
- 1/4 cup dill pickles, diced
- 1 tablespoon fresh dill, chopped
- 8 large lettuce leaves
- 1/4 teaspoon salt
- 1/4 teaspoon black pepper

Directions:

1. In a medium bowl, combine the tuna, Greek yogurt, Dijon mustard, celery, red onion, dill pickles, fresh dill, salt, and black pepper. Mix until well combined.
2. Spoon the tuna salad onto the lettuce leaves, dividing it evenly among them. Serve immediately.

Nutritional Information: 150 calories, 20g protein, 5g carbohydrates, 6g fat, 2g fiber, 30mg cholesterol, 400mg sodium, 300mg potassium.

56. Greek Salad with Feta Cheese

Yield: 4 servings | Prep time: 10 minutes | Cook time: 0 minutes

Ingredients:

- 4 cups chopped romaine lettuce
- 1 cup cherry tomatoes, halved
- 1/2 cucumber, sliced
- 1/4 red onion, thinly sliced
- 1/4 cup Kalamata olives, pitted and halved
- 1/4 cup feta cheese, crumbled
- 2 tablespoons olive oil
- 2 tablespoons red wine vinegar
- 1 teaspoon dried oregano
- 1/4 teaspoon salt
- 1/4 teaspoon black pepper

Directions:

1. In a large bowl, combine the romaine lettuce, cherry tomatoes, cucumber, red onion, and Kalamata olives.
2. In a small bowl, whisk together the olive oil, red wine vinegar, dried oregano, salt, and black pepper.
3. Pour the dressing over the salad and toss to coat. Sprinkle with feta cheese and serve immediately.

Nutritional Information: 200 calories, 6g protein, 10g carbohydrates, 16g fat, 4g fiber, 15mg cholesterol, 500mg sodium, 400mg potassium.

57. Stuffed Bell Peppers with Quinoa

Yield: 4 servings | Prep time: 10 minutes | Cook time: 25 minutes

Ingredients:

- 4 large bell peppers
- 1 cup cooked quinoa
- 1 cup black beans, rinsed and drained
- 1 cup corn kernels
- 1 cup diced tomatoes
- 1/2 cup shredded cheddar cheese
- 1 teaspoon ground cumin
- 1/2 teaspoon salt
- 1/4 teaspoon black pepper
- 1/4 cup chopped fresh cilantro (optional)

Directions:

1. Preheat the oven to 375°F (190°C). Cut the tops off the bell peppers and remove the seeds.
2. In a large bowl, combine the cooked quinoa, black beans, corn, diced tomatoes, ground cumin, salt, and black pepper.
3. Stuff the bell peppers with the quinoa mixture and place them in a baking dish.
4. Cover with aluminum foil and bake for 20 minutes. Remove the foil, sprinkle the tops with shredded cheddar cheese, and bake for an additional 5 minutes, or until the cheese is melted. Garnish with chopped cilantro if desired. Serve warm.

Nutritional Information: 300 calories, 12g protein, 45g carbohydrates, 8g fat, 10g fiber, 15mg cholesterol, 450mg sodium, 800mg potassium.

58. Spinach and Chicken Caesar Wrap

Yield: 4 servings | Prep time: 10 minutes | Cook time: 10 minutes

Ingredients:

- 2 boneless, skinless chicken breasts
- 4 cups spinach leaves
- 1/2 cup Caesar dressing (preferably low-fat)
- 1/4 cup grated Parmesan cheese
- 4 whole grain tortillas
- 1 tablespoon olive oil
- 1/4 teaspoon salt
- 1/4 teaspoon black pepper

Directions:

1. Preheat a grill or skillet over medium-high heat. Season the chicken breasts with salt and black pepper.
2. Grill or cook the chicken for 5-7 minutes on each side, or until fully cooked. Let cool and slice.
3. In a large bowl, toss the spinach leaves with Caesar dressing and grated Parmesan cheese.
4. Divide the spinach mixture and sliced chicken among the tortillas. Roll up the tortillas to form wraps. Serve immediately.

Nutritional Information: 350 calories, 30g protein, 24g carbohydrates, 14g fat, 4g fiber, 60mg cholesterol, 700mg sodium, 600mg potassium.

59. Asian Chicken Lettuce Wraps

Yield: 4 servings | Prep time: 10 minutes | Cook time: 10 minutes

Ingredients:

- 1 pound ground chicken
- 1/2 cup diced onions
- 1/2 cup diced water chestnuts
- 2 cloves garlic, minced
- 2 tablespoons soy sauce (low-sodium)
- 1 tablespoon hoisin sauce
- 1 tablespoon rice vinegar
- 1 teaspoon sesame oil
- 1/4 teaspoon red pepper flakes (optional)
- 8 large lettuce leaves
- 2 tablespoons chopped green onions (optional)

Directions:

1. Heat a large skillet over medium heat. Add the ground chicken and cook until no longer pink, about 5-7 minutes.
2. Add the onions, water chestnuts, and garlic. Cook for an additional 3-4 minutes until the vegetables are tender.
3. Stir in the soy sauce, hoisin sauce, rice vinegar, sesame oil, and red pepper flakes (if using). Cook for another 1-2 minutes until heated through.
4. Spoon the chicken mixture into the lettuce leaves. Garnish with chopped green onions if desired. Serve immediately.

Nutritional Information: 220 calories, 25g protein, 8g carbohydrates, 10g fat, 2g fiber, 80mg cholesterol, 600mg sodium, 400mg potassium.

60. Balsamic Chicken and Vegetables

Yield: 4 servings | Prep time: 10 minutes | Cook time: 25 minutes

Ingredients:

- 2 boneless, skinless chicken breasts
- 1 cup cherry tomatoes, halved
- 1 zucchini, sliced
- 1 red bell pepper, sliced
- 1/4 cup balsamic vinegar
- 2 tablespoons olive oil
- 1 teaspoon dried basil
- 1/4 teaspoon salt
- 1/4 teaspoon black pepper

Directions:

1. Preheat the oven to 400°F (200°C). In a small bowl, whisk together the balsamic vinegar, olive oil, dried basil, salt, and black pepper.
2. Place the chicken breasts in a baking dish. Arrange the cherry tomatoes, zucchini, and red bell pepper around the chicken.
3. Pour the balsamic vinegar mixture over the chicken and vegetables.
4. Bake for 20-25 minutes, or until the chicken is fully cooked and the vegetables are tender. Serve hot.

Nutritional Information: 300 calories, 25g protein, 12g carbohydrates, 14g fat, 3g fiber, 70mg cholesterol, 400mg sodium, 600mg potassium.

61.   Tomato Basil Soup

Yield: 4 servings | Prep time: 10 minutes | Cook time: 30 minutes

Ingredients:

- 1 tablespoon olive oil
- 1 onion, diced
- 2 cloves garlic, minced
- 1 can (28 oz) crushed tomatoes
- 2 cups vegetable broth
- 1/4 cup fresh basil leaves, chopped
- 1/2 teaspoon salt
- 1/4 teaspoon black pepper
- 1/4 cup heavy cream (optional)

Directions:

1. Heat the olive oil in a large pot over medium heat. Add the onion and garlic. Sauté for 5-7 minutes until the onion is soft and translucent.
2. Add the crushed tomatoes, vegetable broth, basil leaves, salt, and black pepper. Bring to a boil, then reduce heat and simmer for 20-25 minutes.
3. If using, stir in the heavy cream and simmer for an additional 2-3 minutes.
4. Use an immersion blender to puree the soup until smooth, or transfer to a blender in batches. Serve hot.

Nutritional Information: 180 calories, 4g protein, 20g carbohydrates, 10g fat, 4g fiber, 10mg cholesterol, 800mg sodium, 700mg potassium.

62.   Eggplant Rollatini

Yield: 4 servings | Prep time: 20 minutes | Cook time: 30 minutes

Ingredients:

- 2 large eggplants, sliced lengthwise
- 1 cup ricotta cheese
- 1/2 cup grated Parmesan cheese
- 1/2 cup shredded mozzarella cheese
- 1 egg, beaten
- 1 cup marinara sauce
- 1/4 cup fresh basil leaves, chopped
- 1 tablespoon olive oil
- 1/4 teaspoon salt
- 1/4 teaspoon black pepper

Directions:

1. Preheat the oven to 375°F (190°C). Brush the eggplant slices with olive oil and season with salt and black pepper.
2. Arrange the eggplant slices on a baking sheet and bake for 15 minutes, or until tender.
3. In a medium bowl, combine the ricotta cheese, Parmesan cheese, shredded mozzarella cheese, beaten egg, and fresh basil. Mix until well combined.
4. Spread a thin layer of marinara sauce in a baking dish. Spoon the cheese mixture onto each eggplant slice and roll up. Place the rolls seam-side down in the baking dish.
5. Top with remaining marinara sauce and bake for 20 minutes, or until the cheese is melted and bubbly. Serve warm.

Nutritional Information: 250 calories, 14g protein, 15g carbohydrates, 15g fat, 6g fiber, 70mg cholesterol, 600mg sodium, 600mg potassium.

63.   Kale and Quinoa Salad

Yield: 4 servings | Prep time: 15 minutes | Cook time: 15 minutes

Ingredients:

- 1 cup quinoa
- 2 cups water
- 4 cups chopped kale
- 1/2 cup dried cranberries
- 1/4 cup sunflower seeds
- 1/4 cup crumbled feta cheese

- 1/4 cup olive oil
- 2 tablespoons lemon juice
- 1 tablespoon apple cider vinegar
- 1 teaspoon honey
- 1/4 teaspoon salt
- 1/4 teaspoon black pepper

Directions:

1. Rinse the quinoa under cold water. In a medium saucepan, bring the quinoa and water to a boil.
2. Reduce the heat to low, cover, and simmer for 15 minutes, or until the water is absorbed and the quinoa is tender. Let cool.
3. In a large bowl, combine the cooked quinoa, chopped kale, dried cranberries, sunflower seeds, and crumbled feta cheese.
4. In a small bowl, whisk together the olive oil, lemon juice, apple cider vinegar, honey, salt, and black pepper. Pour over the salad and toss to coat. Serve immediately.

Nutritional Information: 300 calories, 10g protein, 30g carbohydrates, 16g fat, 5g fiber, 15mg cholesterol, 400mg sodium, 700mg potassium.

64.   Chicken and Avocado Salad

Yield: 4 servings | Prep time: 10 minutes | Cook time: 10 minutes

Ingredients:

- 2 boneless, skinless chicken breasts
- 4 cups mixed greens
- 1 avocado, sliced
- 1/2 cup cherry tomatoes, halved
- 1/4 cup red onion, thinly sliced

- 2 tablespoons olive oil
- 2 tablespoons lemon juice
- 1 teaspoon Dijon mustard
- 1/4 teaspoon salt
- 1/4 teaspoon black pepper

Directions:

1. Preheat a grill or skillet over medium-high heat. Season the chicken breasts with salt and black pepper.
2. Grill or cook the chicken for 5-7 minutes on each side, or until fully cooked. Let cool and slice.
3. In a large bowl, combine the mixed greens, avocado, cherry tomatoes, and red onion.
4. In a small bowl, whisk together the olive oil, lemon juice, Dijon mustard, salt, and black pepper. Drizzle over the salad and toss to coat.
5. Top the salad with the sliced chicken. Serve immediately.

Nutritional Information: 350 calories, 30g protein, 15g carbohydrates, 20g fat, 6g fiber, 60mg cholesterol, 400mg sodium, 600mg potassium.

65.   Turkey Chili

Yield: 6 servings | Prep time: 10 minutes | Cook time: 30 minutes

Ingredients:

- 1 pound ground turkey
- 1 onion, diced
- 2 cloves garlic, minced
- 1 red bell pepper, diced
- 1 green bell pepper, diced
- 1 can (15 oz) kidney beans, rinsed and drained
- 1 can (15 oz) black beans, rinsed and drained
- 1 can (15 oz) diced tomatoes
- 1 can (15 oz) tomato sauce
- 2 tablespoons chili powder
- 1 teaspoon ground cumin
- 1/2 teaspoon salt
- 1/4 teaspoon black pepper
- 2 tablespoons olive oil

Directions:

1. Heat the olive oil in a large pot over medium heat. Add the ground turkey and cook until no longer pink, about 5-7 minutes.
2. Add the onion, garlic, red bell pepper, and green bell pepper. Cook for an additional 5-7 minutes until the vegetables are tender.
3. Stir in the kidney beans, black beans, diced tomatoes, tomato sauce, chili powder, ground cumin, salt, and black pepper. Bring to a boil, then reduce heat and simmer for 20-25 minutes, stirring occasionally. Serve hot.

Nutritional Information: 300 calories, 25g protein, 35g carbohydrates, 10g fat, 10g fiber, 50mg cholesterol, 700mg sodium, 800mg potassium.

66.   Grilled Salmon Salad

Yield: 4 servings | Prep time: 10 minutes | Cook time: 10 minutes

Ingredients:

- 4 salmon fillets (4 oz each)
- 6 cups mixed greens
- 1/2 cup cherry tomatoes, halved
- 1/4 cup red onion, thinly sliced
- 1/4 cup crumbled feta cheese
- 2 tablespoons olive oil
- 2 tablespoons lemon juice
- 1 teaspoon Dijon mustard
- 1/4 teaspoon salt
- 1/4 teaspoon black pepper

Directions:

1. Preheat a grill to medium-high heat. Season the salmon fillets with salt and black pepper.
2. Grill the salmon for 4-5 minutes on each side, or until fully cooked.
3. In a large bowl, combine the mixed greens, cherry tomatoes, red onion, and crumbled feta cheese.
4. In a small bowl, whisk together the olive oil, lemon juice, and Dijon mustard. Drizzle over the salad and toss to coat.
5. Top the salad with the grilled salmon. Serve immediately.

Nutritional Information: 350 calories, 30g protein, 10g carbohydrates, 20g fat, 2g fiber, 60mg cholesterol, 400mg sodium, 600mg potassium.

67.   Chicken and Broccoli Alfredo

Yield: 4 servings | Prep time: 10 minutes | Cook time: 20 minutes

Ingredients:

- 2 boneless, skinless chicken breasts, cut into strips
- 4 cups broccoli florets
- 8 ounces whole grain fettuccine
- 1 cup heavy cream
- 1/2 cup grated Parmesan cheese
- 2 cloves garlic, minced
- 1 tablespoon olive oil
- 1/4 teaspoon salt
- 1/4 teaspoon black pepper
- 1/4 teaspoon red pepper flakes (optional)

Directions:

1. Cook the fettuccine according to the package instructions. Drain and set aside.
2. In a large skillet, heat the olive oil over medium heat. Add the chicken strips and cook until no longer pink, about 5-7 minutes.
3. Add the broccoli florets and garlic. Cook for an additional 3-4 minutes until the broccoli is tender-crisp.
4. Stir in the heavy cream, grated Parmesan cheese, salt, black pepper, and red pepper flakes (if using). Bring to a simmer and cook for 2-3 minutes until the sauce has thickened.
5. Add the cooked fettuccine to the skillet and toss to coat with the sauce. Serve hot.

Nutritional Information: 450 calories, 30g protein, 40g carbohydrates, 20g fat, 6g fiber, 100mg cholesterol, 400mg sodium, 600mg potassium.

68.   Turkey and Zucchini Skillet

Yield: 4 servings | Prep time: 10 minutes | Cook time: 20 minutes

Ingredients:

- 1 pound ground turkey
- 2 medium zucchinis, diced
- 1 red bell pepper, diced
- 1/2 cup diced red onion
- 2 cloves garlic, minced
- 1 tablespoon olive oil
- 1/2 cup low-sodium chicken broth
- 1/4 cup grated Parmesan cheese
- 1 teaspoon Italian seasoning
- 1/4 teaspoon salt
- 1/4 teaspoon black pepper
- 1 tablespoon chopped fresh basil (optional, for garnish)

Directions:

1. In a large skillet, heat olive oil over medium-high heat. Add ground turkey and cook until browned, about 5-7 minutes.
2. Add garlic and diced red onion to the skillet and cook until fragrant, about 2 minutes.
3. Stir in the diced zucchini and red bell pepper. Cook until tender, about 5-7 minutes.
4. Pour in the chicken broth and add Italian seasoning, salt, and black pepper. Simmer for 2-3 minutes.
5. Sprinkle with grated Parmesan cheese and stir until melted and well combined.
6. Serve immediately, garnished with chopped fresh basil if desired.

Nutritional Information: 250 calories, 28g protein, 10g carbohydrates, 12g fat, 3g fiber, 70mg cholesterol, 350mg sodium, 600mg potassium.

69.   Sweet Potato and Black Bean Tacos

Yield: 4 servings | Prep time: 10 minutes | Cook time: 20 minutes

Ingredients:

- 2 medium sweet potatoes, peeled and diced
- 1 can (15 oz) black beans, rinsed and drained
- 1 tablespoon olive oil
- 1 teaspoon ground cumin
- 1/2 teaspoon chili powder
- 1/4 teaspoon salt
- 1/4 teaspoon black pepper
- 8 small corn tortillas
- 1/2 cup diced red onion
- 1/4 cup chopped fresh cilantro
- 1/4 cup crumbled feta cheese (optional)
- Lime wedges for serving (optional)

Directions:

1. Preheat the oven to 400°F (200°C). Place the diced sweet potatoes on a baking sheet and drizzle with olive oil. Sprinkle with ground cumin, chili powder, salt, and black pepper. Toss to coat.
2. Roast the sweet potatoes for 20 minutes, or until tender and slightly caramelized.
3. While the sweet potatoes are roasting, heat the black beans in a small saucepan over medium heat.
4. Warm the tortillas in a dry skillet over medium heat.
5. Assemble the tacos by dividing the roasted sweet potatoes and black beans among the tortillas. Top with diced red onion, chopped cilantro, and crumbled feta cheese if desired. Serve with lime wedges.

Nutritional Information: 300 calories, 10g protein, 50g carbohydrates, 8g fat, 12g fiber, 0mg cholesterol, 400mg sodium, 800mg potassium.

70.   Baked Cod with Asparagus

Yield: 4 servings | Prep time: 10 minutes | Cook time: 20 minutes

Ingredients:

- 4 cod fillets (4 oz each)
- 1 pound asparagus, trimmed
- 2 tablespoons olive oil
- 2 cloves garlic, minced
- 1 lemon, sliced
- 1/4 teaspoon salt
- 1/4 teaspoon black pepper
- 1 tablespoon fresh parsley, chopped (optional)

Directions:

1. Preheat the oven to 400°F (200°C). Line a baking sheet with parchment paper.
2. Place the cod fillets and asparagus on the prepared baking sheet. Drizzle with olive oil and sprinkle with minced garlic, salt, and black pepper.
3. Arrange the lemon slices on top of the cod fillets.
4. Bake for 15-20 minutes, or until the cod is opaque and flakes easily with a fork and the asparagus is tender. Garnish with fresh parsley if desired. Serve warm.

Nutritional Information: 200 calories, 25g protein, 8g carbohydrates, 8g fat, 3g fiber, 60mg cholesterol, 400mg sodium, 600mg potassium.

71. Stuffed Portobello Mushrooms

Yield: 4 servings | Prep time: 10 minutes | Cook time: 25 minutes

Ingredients:

- 4 large portobello mushrooms
- 1 cup fresh spinach, chopped
- 1/2 cup cherry tomatoes, halved
- 1/2 cup shredded mozzarella cheese
- 1/4 cup grated Parmesan cheese
- 2 cloves garlic, minced
- 1 tablespoon olive oil
- 1/4 teaspoon salt
- 1/4 teaspoon black pepper

Directions:

1. Preheat the oven to 375°F (190°C). Remove the stems from the portobello mushrooms and scoop out the gills.
2. In a large skillet, heat the olive oil over medium heat. Add the garlic and cook for 1-2 minutes until fragrant.
3. Add the chopped spinach and cherry tomatoes. Cook for 3-4 minutes until the spinach is wilted and the tomatoes are slightly softened. Season with salt and black pepper.
4. Place the portobello mushrooms on a baking sheet. Divide the spinach mixture among the mushrooms. Top with shredded mozzarella cheese and grated Parmesan cheese.
5. Bake for 20-25 minutes, or until the mushrooms are tender and the cheese is melted and bubbly. Serve warm.

Nutritional Information: 200 calories, 10g protein, 10g carbohydrates, 14g fat, 3g fiber, 20mg cholesterol, 400mg sodium, 500mg potassium.

72. Eggplant Lasagna

Yield: 4 servings | Prep time: 15 minutes | Cook time: 30 minutes

Ingredients:

- 2 large eggplants, sliced lengthwise
- 1 pound ground turkey
- 1 cup marinara sauce (low-sugar)
- 1 cup ricotta cheese
- 1/2 cup shredded mozzarella cheese
- 1/4 cup grated Parmesan cheese
- 2 cloves garlic, minced
- 1 tablespoon olive oil
- 1 teaspoon dried oregano
- 1/4 teaspoon salt
- 1/4 teaspoon black pepper

Directions:

1. Preheat the oven to 375°F (190°C).
2. In a skillet, heat olive oil over medium heat. Add garlic and cook until fragrant, about 1 minute.
3. Add ground turkey, oregano, salt, and pepper. Cook until browned, about 5-7 minutes.
4. In a baking dish, layer eggplant slices, cooked turkey, marinara sauce, and ricotta cheese. Repeat layers.
5. Top with shredded mozzarella and Parmesan cheese.
6. Bake for 25-30 minutes, until cheese is bubbly and golden. Serve hot.

Nutritional Information: 280 calories, 25g protein, 12g carbohydrates, 15g fat, 4g fiber, 70mg cholesterol, 500mg sodium, 600mg potassium.

73.   Turkey and Spinach Stuffed Peppers

Yield: 4 servings | Prep time: 10 minutes | Cook time: 25 minutes

Ingredients:

- 4 large bell peppers
- 1 pound ground turkey
- 2 cups fresh spinach, chopped
- 1/2 cup diced tomatoes
- 1/4 cup diced onions

- 1/2 cup shredded mozzarella cheese
- 1 teaspoon ground cumin
- 1/2 teaspoon salt
- 1/4 teaspoon black pepper
- 1 tablespoon olive oil

Directions:

1. Preheat the oven to 375°F (190°C). Cut the tops off the bell peppers and remove the seeds.
2. In a large skillet, heat the olive oil over medium heat. Add the ground turkey, diced onions, salt, and black pepper. Cook until the turkey is no longer pink, about 5-7 minutes.
3. Stir in the chopped spinach, diced tomatoes, and ground cumin. Cook for an additional 3-4 minutes until the spinach is wilted.
4. Stuff the bell peppers with the turkey mixture and place them in a baking dish. Top with shredded mozzarella cheese.
5. Cover with aluminum foil and bake for 20 minutes. Remove the foil and bake for an additional 5 minutes, or until the cheese is melted. Serve warm.

Nutritional Information: 300 calories, 25g protein, 15g carbohydrates, 15g fat, 3g fiber, 60mg cholesterol, 500mg sodium, 700mg potassium.

74.   Pasta Salad with Veggies and Feta

Yield: 4 servings | Prep time: 10 minutes | Cook time: 10 minutes

Ingredients:

- 8 ounces whole grain pasta
- 1 cup cherry tomatoes, halved
- 1 cup diced cucumber
- 1/2 cup diced red bell pepper
- 1/4 cup diced red onion
- 1/4 cup crumbled feta cheese

- 1/4 cup olive oil
- 2 tablespoons red wine vinegar
- 1 teaspoon dried oregano
- 1/4 teaspoon salt
- 1/4 teaspoon black pepper

Directions:

1. Cook the pasta according to the package instructions. Drain and rinse under cold water to cool.
2. In a large bowl, combine the cooked pasta, cherry tomatoes, cucumber, red bell pepper, red onion, and crumbled feta cheese.
3. In a small bowl, whisk together the olive oil, red wine vinegar, dried oregano, salt, and black pepper. Pour over the pasta salad and toss to coat. Serve immediately or refrigerate for later.

Nutritional Information: 300 calories, 10g protein, 40g carbohydrates, 12g fat, 5g fiber, 10mg cholesterol, 400mg sodium, 300mg potassium.

75.   Zoodle Salad with Avocado Dressing

Yield: 4 servings | Prep time: 10 minutes | Cook time: 0 minutes

Ingredients:

- 4 medium zucchinis, spiralized
- 1 avocado, peeled and pitted
- 1/4 cup Greek yogurt
- 2 tablespoons lime juice
- 1 tablespoon olive oil

- 1 clove garlic, minced
- 1/4 teaspoon salt
- 1/4 teaspoon black pepper
- 1/4 cup chopped fresh cilantro

Directions:

1. In a blender, combine the avocado, Greek yogurt, lime juice, olive oil, garlic, salt, and black pepper. Blend until smooth.
2. In a large bowl, toss the spiralized zucchini noodles with the avocado dressing. Sprinkle with chopped fresh cilantro. Serve immediately.

Nutritional Information: 200 calories, 5g protein, 15g carbohydrates, 14g fat, 6g fiber, 0mg cholesterol, 300mg sodium, 700mg potassium.

76.   Spicy Shrimp and Avocado Salad

Yield: 4 servings | Prep time: 10 minutes | Cook time: 5 minutes

Ingredients:

- 1 pound large shrimp, peeled and deveined
- 1 tablespoon olive oil
- 1 teaspoon chili powder
- 1/4 teaspoon salt
- 1/4 teaspoon black pepper
- 6 cups mixed greens

- 1 avocado, sliced
- 1/2 cup cherry tomatoes, halved
- 1/4 cup red onion, thinly sliced
- 1/4 cup fresh cilantro, chopped
- 2 tablespoons lime juice

Directions:

1. In a large skillet, heat the olive oil over medium-high heat. Add the shrimp, chili powder, salt, and black pepper. Cook for 2-3 minutes on each side, or until the shrimp are pink and opaque.
2. In a large bowl, combine the mixed greens, avocado, cherry tomatoes, red onion, and fresh cilantro.
3. Add the cooked shrimp to the salad. Drizzle with lime juice and toss to coat. Serve immediately.

Nutritional Information: 250 calories, 20g protein, 10g carbohydrates, 15g fat, 4g fiber, 170mg cholesterol, 600mg sodium, 600mg potassium.

77.   Mushroom and Spinach Stuffed Chicken Breast

Yield: 4 servings | Prep time: 15 minutes | Cook time: 25 minutes

Ingredients:

- 4 boneless, skinless chicken breasts
- 1 cup fresh spinach, chopped
- 1 cup mushrooms, sliced
- 1/2 cup shredded mozzarella cheese

- 2 cloves garlic, minced
- 1 tablespoon olive oil
- 1/4 teaspoon salt
- 1/4 teaspoon black pepper

Directions:

1. Preheat the oven to 375°F (190°C). Slice each chicken breast horizontally to create a pocket.
2. In a large skillet, heat the olive oil over medium heat. Add the garlic and cook for 1-2 minutes until fragrant.
3. Add the spinach and mushrooms. Cook for 3-4 minutes until the spinach is wilted and the mushrooms are tender. Season with salt and black pepper.
4. Stuff each chicken breast with the spinach and mushroom mixture. Place the stuffed chicken breasts in a baking dish and top with shredded mozzarella cheese.
5. Bake for 20-25 minutes, or until the chicken is fully cooked and the cheese is melted and bubbly. Serve warm.

Nutritional Information: 300 calories, 30g protein, 5g carbohydrates, 16g fat, 2g fiber, 80mg cholesterol, 400mg sodium, 500mg potassium.

78.   Tomato and Mozzarella Stuffed Chicken

Yield: 4 servings | Prep time: 15 minutes | Cook time: 30 minutes

Ingredients:

- 4 boneless, skinless chicken breasts
- 1 cup cherry tomatoes, halved
- 1 cup shredded mozzarella cheese
- 1/4 cup fresh basil leaves, chopped

- 2 cloves garlic, minced
- 1 tablespoon olive oil
- 1/4 teaspoon salt
- 1/4 teaspoon black pepper

Directions:

1. Preheat the oven to 375°F (190°C). Slice each chicken breast horizontally to create a pocket.
2. In a medium bowl, combine the cherry tomatoes, mozzarella cheese, fresh basil, and garlic. Mix well.
3. Stuff each chicken breast with the tomato and mozzarella mixture. Secure with toothpicks if necessary.
4. Heat the olive oil in a large skillet over medium-high heat. Sear the chicken breasts for 2-3 minutes on each side until golden brown.
5. Transfer the seared chicken breasts to a baking dish and bake for 20-25 minutes, or until the chicken is fully cooked. Serve warm.

Nutritional Information: 320 calories, 35g protein, 6g carbohydrates, 18g fat, 1g fiber, 90mg cholesterol, 450mg sodium, 600mg potassium.

79.   Asian Beef and Broccoli Stir-Fry

Yield: 4 servings | Prep time: 10 minutes | Cook time: 15 minutes

Ingredients:

- 1 pound beef sirloin, thinly sliced
- 4 cups broccoli florets
- 1 red bell pepper, sliced
- 1 onion, sliced
- 2 cloves garlic, minced
- 1 tablespoon fresh ginger, grated
- 3 tablespoons soy sauce (low-sodium)
- 1 tablespoon hoisin sauce
- 1 tablespoon sesame oil
- 1/4 teaspoon red pepper flakes (optional)

Directions:

1. In a large skillet or wok, heat the sesame oil over medium-high heat. Add the beef slices and cook until browned, about 5-7 minutes. Remove from the skillet and set aside.
2. In the same skillet, add the broccoli, red bell pepper, onion, garlic, and ginger. Sauté for 5-7 minutes until the vegetables are tender-crisp.
3. Return the beef to the skillet. Stir in the soy sauce, hoisin sauce, and red pepper flakes (if using). Cook for another 2-3 minutes until heated through. Serve hot.

Nutritional Information: 320 calories, 28g protein, 18g carbohydrates, 16g fat, 4g fiber, 70mg cholesterol, 600mg sodium, 700mg potassium.

80.   Quinoa Stuffed Acorn Squash

Yield: 4 servings | Prep time: 15 minutes | Cook time: 45 minutes

Ingredients:

- 2 acorn squashes, halved and seeded
- 1 cup cooked quinoa
- 1/2 cup dried cranberries
- 1/2 cup chopped pecans
- 1/4 cup fresh parsley, chopped
- 1/4 cup feta cheese, crumbled
- 2 tablespoons olive oil
- 1 tablespoon maple syrup
- 1/4 teaspoon salt
- 1/4 teaspoon black pepper

Directions:

1. Preheat the oven to 400°F (200°C). Place the acorn squash halves cut side up on a baking sheet. Drizzle with 1 tablespoon of olive oil and season with salt and black pepper. Roast for 40-45 minutes, or until tender.
2. In a large bowl, combine the cooked quinoa, dried cranberries, chopped pecans, fresh parsley, feta cheese, maple syrup, and the remaining tablespoon of olive oil. Mix well.
3. Spoon the quinoa mixture into the roasted acorn squash halves. Serve warm.

Nutritional Information: 350 calories, 8g protein, 45g carbohydrates, 18g fat, 6g fiber, 10mg cholesterol, 300mg sodium, 800mg potassium.

Delicious Dinners for Diabetics

81.   Baked Salmon with Asparagus

Yield: 4 servings | Prep time: 10 minutes | Cook time: 15 minutes

Ingredients:

- 4 salmon fillets (4 oz each)
- 1 pound asparagus, trimmed
- 2 tablespoons olive oil
- 1 lemon, sliced

- 2 cloves garlic, minced
- 1/4 teaspoon salt
- 1/4 teaspoon black pepper
- 1 tablespoon fresh dill, chopped (optional)

Directions:

1. Preheat the oven to 400°F (200°C). Line a baking sheet with parchment paper.
2. Arrange the salmon fillets and asparagus on the prepared baking sheet. Drizzle with olive oil and sprinkle with minced garlic, salt, and black pepper.
3. Place the lemon slices on top of the salmon fillets.
4. Bake for 12-15 minutes, or until the salmon is opaque and flakes easily with a fork and the asparagus is tender. Garnish with fresh dill if desired. Serve warm.

Nutritional Information: 350 calories, 30g protein, 8g carbohydrates, 22g fat, 3g fiber, 70mg cholesterol, 400mg sodium, 600mg potassium.

82.   Grilled Chicken with Steamed Vegetables

Ingredients:

- 4 boneless, skinless chicken breasts
- 2 cups broccoli florets
- 2 cups sliced carrots
- 2 cups green beans, trimmed
- 2 tablespoons olive oil

-
- 1 tablespoon lemon juice
- 1 teaspoon dried thyme
- 1/4 teaspoon salt
- 1/4 teaspoon black pepper

Directions:

1. Preheat a grill to medium-high heat. Season the chicken breasts with salt, black pepper, and dried thyme.
2. Grill the chicken for 5-7 minutes on each side, or until fully cooked. Remove from the grill and drizzle with lemon juice.
3. While the chicken is grilling, steam the broccoli, carrots, and green beans until tender, about 5-7 minutes.
4. Divide the grilled chicken and steamed vegetables among four plates. Drizzle with olive oil. Serve warm.

Nutritional Information: 300 calories, 30g protein, 15g carbohydrates, 14g fat, 6g fiber, 80mg cholesterol, 400mg sodium, 700mg potassium.

83.   Beef and Broccoli Stir-Fry

Yield: 4 servings | Prep time: 10 minutes | Cook time: 15 minutes

Ingredients:

- 1 pound beef sirloin, thinly sliced
- 4 cups broccoli florets
- 1 red bell pepper, sliced
- 1 onion, sliced
- 2 cloves garlic, minced
- 1 tablespoon fresh ginger, grated
- 3 tablespoons soy sauce (low-sodium)
- 1 tablespoon hoisin sauce
- 1 tablespoon sesame oil
- 1/4 teaspoon red pepper flakes (optional)

Directions:

1. In a large skillet or wok, heat the sesame oil over medium-high heat. Add the beef slices and cook until browned, about 5-7 minutes. Remove from the skillet and set aside.
2. In the same skillet, add the broccoli, red bell pepper, onion, garlic, and ginger. Sauté for 5-7 minutes until the vegetables are tender-crisp.
3. Return the beef to the skillet. Stir in the soy sauce, hoisin sauce, and red pepper flakes (if using). Cook for another 2-3 minutes until heated through. Serve hot.

Nutritional Information: 320 calories, 28g protein, 18g carbohydrates, 16g fat, 4g fiber, 70mg cholesterol, 600mg sodium, 700mg potassium.

84.   Lemon Garlic Shrimp with Zoodles

Yield: 4 servings | Prep time: 10 minutes | Cook time: 10 minutes

Ingredients:

- 1 pound large shrimp, peeled and deveined
- 4 medium zucchinis, spiralized
- 2 cloves garlic, minced
- 2 tablespoons olive oil
- 1 lemon, juiced and zested
- 1/4 teaspoon salt
- 1/4 teaspoon black pepper
- 1/4 cup fresh parsley, chopped (optional)

Directions:

1. In a large skillet, heat the olive oil over medium-high heat. Add the garlic and cook for 1-2 minutes until fragrant.
2. Add the shrimp, salt, and black pepper. Cook for 2-3 minutes on each side, or until the shrimp are pink and opaque.
3. Stir in the lemon juice and zest. Remove the shrimp from the skillet and set aside.
4. In the same skillet, add the spiralized zucchini noodles. Cook for 2-3 minutes until just tender.
5. Return the shrimp to the skillet and toss to combine with the zoodles. Garnish with fresh parsley if desired. Serve immediately.

Nutritional Information: 250 calories, 25g protein, 10g carbohydrates, 12g fat, 4g fiber, 170mg cholesterol, 600mg sodium, 700mg potassium.

85.   Spaghetti Squash with Turkey Meatballs

Yield: 4 servings | Prep time: 20 minutes | Cook time: 40 minutes

Ingredients:

- 1 large spaghetti squash
- 1 pound ground turkey
- 1/2 cup breadcrumbs (whole grain if possible)
- 1/4 cup grated Parmesan cheese
- 1 egg, beaten
- 2 cloves garlic, minced
- 1 teaspoon dried oregano
- 1 teaspoon dried basil
- 1/4 teaspoon salt
- 1/4 teaspoon black pepper
- 2 cups marinara sauce

Directions:

1. Preheat the oven to 400°F (200°C). Cut the spaghetti squash in half lengthwise and remove the seeds.
2. Place the squash halves cut side down on a baking sheet and bake for 35-40 minutes, or until the squash is tender.
3. While the squash is baking, in a large bowl, combine the ground turkey, breadcrumbs, grated Parmesan cheese, beaten egg, minced garlic, dried oregano, dried basil, salt, and black pepper. Mix until well combined.
4. Form the mixture into meatballs and place them on a separate baking sheet. Bake for 20 minutes, or until fully cooked.
5. Heat the marinara sauce in a saucepan over medium heat. Add the cooked meatballs and simmer for 5 minutes.
6. When the squash is done, use a fork to scrape out the flesh into spaghetti-like strands. Divide the strands among four plates and top with the turkey meatballs and marinara sauce. Serve warm.

Nutritional Information: 350 calories, 30g protein, 25g carbohydrates, 12g fat, 6g fiber, 100mg cholesterol, 700mg sodium, 800mg potassium.

86.   Chicken Fajita Bowl

Yield: 4 servings | Prep time: 10 minutes | Cook time: 20 minutes

Ingredients:

- 2 boneless, skinless chicken breasts, thinly sliced
- 1 red bell pepper, sliced
- 1 green bell pepper, sliced
- 1 yellow bell pepper, sliced
- 1 onion, sliced
- 2 tablespoons olive oil
- 2 cloves garlic, minced
- 1 teaspoon ground cumin
- 1 teaspoon chili powder
- 1/4 teaspoon salt
- 1/4 teaspoon black pepper
- 4 cups cooked brown rice
- 1/4 cup fresh cilantro, chopped (optional)
- Lime wedges for serving

Directions:

1. In a large skillet, heat the olive oil over medium-high heat. Add the sliced chicken, minced garlic, ground cumin, chili powder, salt, and black pepper. Cook for 5-7 minutes until the chicken is fully cooked.
2. Add the sliced bell peppers and onion to the skillet. Cook for another 5-7 minutes until the vegetables are tender-crisp.
3. Divide the cooked brown rice among four bowls. Top with the chicken and vegetable mixture. Garnish with fresh cilantro and serve with lime wedges.

Nutritional Information: 400 calories, 30g protein, 45g carbohydrates, 12g fat, 6g fiber, 80mg cholesterol, 400mg sodium, 700mg potassium.

87.   Stuffed Bell Peppers with Ground Turkey

Yield: 4 servings | Prep time: 15 minutes | Cook time: 25 minutes

Ingredients:

- 4 large bell peppers
- 1 pound ground turkey
- 1 cup cooked brown rice
- 1/2 cup diced tomatoes
- 1/4 cup diced onions

- 1/2 cup shredded mozzarella cheese
- 1 teaspoon ground cumin
- 1/2 teaspoon salt
- 1/4 teaspoon black pepper
- 1 tablespoon olive oil

Directions:

1. Preheat the oven to 375°F (190°C). Cut the tops off the bell peppers and remove the seeds.
2. In a large skillet, heat the olive oil over medium heat. Add the ground turkey, diced onions, salt, and black pepper. Cook until the turkey is no longer pink, about 5-7 minutes.
3. Stir in the cooked brown rice, diced tomatoes, and ground cumin. Cook for an additional 3-4 minutes until well combined.
4. Stuff the bell peppers with the turkey mixture and place them in a baking dish. Top with shredded mozzarella cheese.
5. Cover with aluminum foil and bake for 20 minutes. Remove the foil and bake for an additional 5 minutes, or until the cheese is melted. Serve warm.

Nutritional Information: 320 calories, 25g protein, 25g carbohydrates, 12g fat, 5g fiber, 60mg cholesterol, 500mg sodium, 700mg potassium.

88.   Grilled Tuna with Mango Salsa

Yield: 4 servings | Prep time: 10 minutes | Cook time: 10 minutes

Ingredients:

- 4 tuna steaks (4 oz each)
- 1 mango, peeled and diced
- 1/2 red bell pepper, diced
- 1/4 red onion, diced
- 1/4 cup fresh cilantro, chopped

- 1 jalapeño, seeded and minced
- 2 tablespoons lime juice
- 2 tablespoons olive oil
- 1/4 teaspoon salt
- 1/4 teaspoon black pepper

Directions:

1. In a medium bowl, combine the diced mango, red bell pepper, red onion, fresh cilantro, jalapeño, lime juice, salt, and black pepper. Mix well and set aside.
2. Preheat a grill to medium-high heat. Brush the tuna steaks with olive oil and season with salt and black pepper.
3. Grill the tuna steaks for 2-3 minutes on each side, or until desired doneness.
4. Serve the grilled tuna topped with mango salsa. Serve immediately.

Nutritional Information: 300 calories, 30g protein, 15g carbohydrates, 12g fat, 2g fiber, 70mg cholesterol, 400mg sodium, 700mg potassium.

89.   Chicken and Spinach Stuffed Portobellos

Yield: 4 servings | Prep time: 10 minutes | Cook time: 25 minutes

Ingredients:

- 4 large portobello mushrooms
- 2 boneless, skinless chicken breasts, diced
- 2 cups fresh spinach, chopped
- 1/2 cup shredded mozzarella cheese

- 2 cloves garlic, minced
- 1 tablespoon olive oil
- 1/4 teaspoon salt
- 1/4 teaspoon black pepper

Directions:

1. Preheat the oven to 375°F (190°C). Remove the stems from the portobello mushrooms and scoop out the gills.
2. In a large skillet, heat the olive oil over medium heat. Add the garlic and cook for 1-2 minutes until fragrant.
3. Add the diced chicken, salt, and black pepper. Cook until the chicken is no longer pink, about 5-7 minutes.
4. Stir in the chopped spinach and cook for another 2-3 minutes until wilted.
5. Place the portobello mushrooms on a baking sheet. Divide the chicken and spinach mixture among the mushrooms and top with shredded mozzarella cheese.
6. Bake for 20-25 minutes, or until the mushrooms are tender and the cheese is melted and bubbly. Serve warm.

Nutritional Information: 300 calories, 25g protein, 10g carbohydrates, 16g fat, 2g fiber, 60mg cholesterol, 500mg sodium.

90.   Grilled Pork Chops with Apple Slaw

Yield: 4 servings | Prep time: 15 minutes | Cook time: 15 minutes

Ingredients:

- 4 boneless pork chops (4 oz each)
- 2 apples, julienned
- 1/2 head red cabbage, shredded
- 1/4 cup apple cider vinegar
- 2 tablespoons olive oil

- 1 tablespoon Dijon mustard
- 1 tablespoon honey
- 1/4 teaspoon salt
- 1/4 teaspoon black pepper
- 1/4 teaspoon smoked paprika

Directions:

1. Preheat a grill to medium-high heat. Season the pork chops with salt, black pepper, and smoked paprika.
2. Grill the pork chops for 5-7 minutes on each side, or until fully cooked.
3. In a large bowl, combine the julienned apples and shredded red cabbage.
4. In a small bowl, whisk together the apple cider vinegar, olive oil, Dijon mustard, honey, salt, and black pepper. Pour over the apple and cabbage mixture and toss to coat.
5. Serve the grilled pork chops with the apple slaw on the side.

Nutritional Information: 300 calories, 25g protein, 20g carbohydrates, 14g fat, 4g fiber, 70mg cholesterol, 400mg sodium, 500mg potassium.

91. Cauliflower Crust Pizza

Yield: 4 servings | Prep time: 20 minutes | Cook time: 25 minutes

Ingredients:

- 1 large head cauliflower, grated
- 1 cup shredded mozzarella cheese
- 1/4 cup grated Parmesan cheese
- 1 egg, beaten
- 1 teaspoon dried oregano
- 1/2 teaspoon garlic powder
- 1/4 teaspoon salt
- 1/4 teaspoon black pepper
- 1/2 cup marinara sauce
- 1 cup cherry tomatoes, halved
- 1/2 cup fresh basil leaves, chopped
- 1/4 cup sliced black olives (optional)

Directions:

1. Preheat the oven to 425°F (220°C). Line a baking sheet with parchment paper.
2. In a large bowl, combine the grated cauliflower, 1/2 cup of the shredded mozzarella cheese, grated Parmesan cheese, beaten egg, dried oregano, garlic powder, salt, and black pepper. Mix until well combined.
3. Press the cauliflower mixture into a 10-inch circle on the prepared baking sheet. Bake for 20 minutes, or until golden brown and firm.
4. Spread the marinara sauce over the cauliflower crust. Top with the remaining shredded mozzarella cheese, cherry tomatoes, fresh basil, and sliced black olives if desired.
5. Bake for an additional 5-7 minutes, or until the cheese is melted and bubbly. Serve warm.

Nutritional Information: 250 calories, 15g protein, 15g carbohydrates, 14g fat, 4g fiber, 70mg cholesterol, 600mg sodium, 700mg potassium.

92. Garlic and Herb Roasted Chicken

Yield: 4 servings | Prep time: 10 minutes | Cook time: 50 minutes

Ingredients:

- 1 whole chicken (about 4 pounds)
- 1/4 cup olive oil
- 4 cloves garlic, minced
- 1 tablespoon fresh rosemary, chopped
- 1 tablespoon fresh thyme, chopped
- 1 lemon, sliced
- 1/4 teaspoon salt
- 1/4 teaspoon black pepper

Directions:

1. Preheat the oven to 375°F (190°C). Place the chicken in a roasting pan.
2. In a small bowl, combine the olive oil, minced garlic, fresh rosemary, fresh thyme, salt, and black pepper.
3. Rub the herb mixture all over the chicken, including under the skin. Arrange the lemon slices around the chicken.
4. Roast for 45-50 minutes, or until the chicken reaches an internal temperature of 165°F (75°C). Let the chicken rest for 10 minutes before carving. Serve warm.

Nutritional Information: 450 calories, 35g protein, 1g carbohydrates, 34g fat, 0g fiber, 120mg cholesterol, 400mg sodium, 400mg potassium.

93.   Vegetarian Chili

Yield: 6 servings | Prep time: 10 minutes | Cook time: 30 minutes

Ingredients:

- 1 tablespoon olive oil
- 1 onion, diced
- 2 cloves garlic, minced
- 1 red bell pepper, diced
- 1 green bell pepper, diced
- 2 carrots, diced
- 1 zucchini, diced
- 1 can (15 oz) kidney beans, rinsed and drained
- 1 can (15 oz) black beans, rinsed and drained
- 1 can (15 oz) diced tomatoes
- 1 can (15 oz) tomato sauce
- 2 tablespoons chili powder
- 1 teaspoon ground cumin
- 1/2 teaspoon smoked paprika
- 1/4 teaspoon salt
- 1/4 teaspoon black pepper
- 1/4 cup fresh cilantro, chopped (optional)

Directions:

1. Heat the olive oil in a large pot over medium heat. Add the onion, garlic, red bell pepper, green bell pepper, and carrots. Sauté for 5-7 minutes until softened.
2. Add the zucchini and cook for another 3-4 minutes.
3. Stir in the kidney beans, black beans, diced tomatoes, tomato sauce, chili powder, ground cumin, smoked paprika, salt, and black pepper. Bring to a boil, then reduce heat and simmer for 25-30 minutes, stirring occasionally.
4. Garnish with fresh cilantro if desired. Serve hot.

Nutritional Information: 280 calories, 12g protein, 50g carbohydrates, 6g fat, 14g fiber, 0mg cholesterol, 600mg sodium, 700mg potassium.

94.   Pesto Zoodle Bowl with Cherry Tomatoes

Yield: 4 servings | Prep time: 10 minutes | Cook time: 10 minutes

Ingredients:

- 4 medium zucchinis, spiralized
- 1 cup cherry tomatoes, halved
- 1/2 cup basil pesto (store-bought or homemade)
- 1/4 cup grated Parmesan cheese
- 1 tablespoon olive oil
- 1/4 teaspoon salt
- 1/4 teaspoon black pepper
- 1/4 cup fresh basil leaves, chopped (optional)

Directions:

1. In a large skillet, heat the olive oil over medium-high heat. Add the spiralized zucchini noodles and cook for 2-3 minutes until just tender.
2. Add the cherry tomatoes, basil pesto, salt, and black pepper. Toss to combine and cook for another 1-2 minutes until heated through.
3. Serve the zucchini noodles topped with grated Parmesan cheese and fresh basil leaves if desired. Serve immediately.

Nutritional Information: 200 calories, 6g protein, 10g carbohydrates, 16g fat, 3g fiber, 10mg cholesterol, 400mg sodium, 600mg potassium.

95.   Turkey and Zucchini Lasagna

Yield: 6 servings | Prep time: 20 minutes | Cook time: 45 minutes

Ingredients:
- 2 large zucchinis, sliced lengthwise into thin strips
- 1 pound ground turkey
- 1 onion, diced
- 2 cloves garlic, minced
- 2 cups marinara sauce
- 1 cup ricotta cheese
- 1 cup shredded mozzarella cheese
- 1/4 cup grated Parmesan cheese
- 1 egg, beaten
- 1 tablespoon olive oil
- 1 teaspoon dried basil
- 1 teaspoon dried oregano
- 1/2 teaspoon salt
- 1/4 teaspoon black pepper

Directions:

1. Preheat the oven to 375°F (190°C). Heat the olive oil in a large skillet over medium heat. Add the ground turkey, onion, garlic, salt, and black pepper. Cook until the turkey is no longer pink, about 5-7 minutes.
2. Stir in the marinara sauce, dried basil, and dried oregano. Simmer for 5 minutes.
3. In a medium bowl, mix the ricotta cheese, grated Parmesan cheese, and beaten egg until well combined.
4. In a 9x13 inch baking dish, layer the zucchini slices, turkey mixture, and ricotta mixture. Repeat the layers until all the ingredients are used, ending with a layer of shredded mozzarella cheese.
5. Cover with aluminum foil and bake for 30 minutes. Remove the foil and bake for an additional 15 minutes, or until the cheese is melted and bubbly. Let stand for 10 minutes before serving.

Nutritional Information: 350 calories, 30g protein, 12g carbohydrates, 20g fat, 3g fiber, 90mg cholesterol, 700mg sodium, 800mg potassium.

96.   Chicken Piccata

Yield: 4 servings | Prep time: 10 minutes | Cook time: 15 minutes

Ingredients:
- 4 boneless, skinless chicken breasts
- 1/4 cup flour
- 1/4 cup chicken broth
- 1/4 cup lemon juice
- 2 tablespoons capers, rinsed
- 2 tablespoons olive oil
- 1 tablespoon butter
- 1/4 teaspoon salt
- 1/4 teaspoon black pepper
- 1/4 cup fresh parsley, chopped (optional)

Directions:

1. Flatten the chicken breasts to an even thickness. Season with salt and black pepper and dredge in flour.
2. In a large skillet, heat the olive oil and butter over medium-high heat. Add the chicken breasts and cook for 3-4 minutes on each side, or until golden brown and fully cooked. Remove from the skillet and set aside.
3. In the same skillet, add the chicken broth, lemon juice, and capers. Bring to a simmer and cook for 2-3 minutes, scraping up any browned bits from the bottom of the skillet.
4. Return the chicken to the skillet and spoon the sauce over the top. Cook for another 2-3 minutes until heated through. Garnish with fresh parsley if desired. Serve immediately.

Nutritional Information: 300 calories, 30g protein, 10g carbohydrates, 14g fat, 1g fiber, 80mg cholesterol, 400mg sodium, 500mg potassium.

97. Eggplant Parmesan

Yield: 4 servings | Prep time: 20 minutes | Cook time: 30 minutes

Ingredients:

- 2 large eggplants, sliced into rounds
- 2 cups marinara sauce
- 1 cup shredded mozzarella cheese
- 1/2 cup grated Parmesan cheese
- 1 cup whole wheat breadcrumbs
- 2 eggs, beaten
- 1/4 cup flour
- 1 tablespoon olive oil
- 1 teaspoon dried basil
- 1 teaspoon dried oregano
- 1/4 teaspoon salt
- 1/4 teaspoon black pepper

Directions:

1. Preheat the oven to 375°F (190°C). Line a baking sheet with parchment paper.
2. In a shallow bowl, mix the whole wheat breadcrumbs, grated Parmesan cheese, dried basil, dried oregano, salt, and black pepper.
3. Dredge each eggplant slice in flour, then dip in beaten eggs, and coat with the breadcrumb mixture.
4. Arrange the breaded eggplant slices on the prepared baking sheet. Drizzle with olive oil and bake for 20 minutes, or until golden brown and crispy.
5. In a baking dish, spread a thin layer of marinara sauce. Layer the eggplant slices, marinara sauce, and shredded mozzarella cheese. Repeat the layers until all the ingredients are used, ending with a layer of mozzarella cheese.
6. Bake for an additional 10 minutes, or until the cheese is melted and bubbly. Serve warm.

Nutritional Information: 300 calories, 12g protein, 30g carbohydrates, 16g fat, 6g fiber, 70mg cholesterol, 600mg sodium, 800mg potassium.

98. Mushroom and Chicken Risotto

Yield: 4 servings | Prep time: 10 minutes | Cook time: 30 minutes

Ingredients:

- 1 cup Arborio rice
- 2 boneless, skinless chicken breasts, diced
- 1 cup mushrooms, sliced
- 1 onion, diced
- 2 cloves garlic, minced
- 4 cups chicken broth
- 1/2 cup grated Parmesan cheese
- 1/4 cup white wine (optional)
- 2 tablespoons olive oil
- 1 tablespoon butter
- 1/4 teaspoon salt
- 1/4 teaspoon black pepper
- 1/4 cup fresh parsley, chopped

Directions:

1. In a large skillet, heat 1 tablespoon of olive oil over medium heat. Add the diced chicken, salt, and black pepper. Cook until the chicken is no longer pink, about 5-7 minutes. Remove from the skillet and set aside.
2. In the same skillet, add the remaining olive oil and butter. Add the onion and garlic and cook for 2-3 minutes until softened.
3. Add the sliced mushrooms and cook for another 3-4 minutes until browned.
4. Stir in the Arborio rice and cook for 1-2 minutes until lightly toasted. If using, add the white wine and cook until evaporated.
5. Gradually add the chicken broth, one cup at a time, stirring frequently until the liquid is absorbed before adding more.
6. Continue cooking and stirring for 18-20 minutes, or until the rice is creamy and tender. Stir in the cooked chicken and grated Parmesan cheese. Garnish with fresh parsley. Serve warm.

Nutritional Information: 400 calories, 25g protein, 50g carbohydrates, 12g fat, 2g fiber, 80mg cholesterol, 600mg sodium, 500mg potassium.

99.   Salmon and Avocado Salad

Yield: 4 servings | Prep time: 10 minutes | Cook time: 10 minutes

Ingredients:

- 4 salmon fillets (4 oz each)
- 6 cups mixed greens
- 1 avocado, sliced
- 1/2 cup cherry tomatoes, halved
- 1/4 cup red onion, thinly sliced

- 1/4 cup olive oil
- 2 tablespoons lemon juice
- 1 teaspoon Dijon mustard
- 1/4 teaspoon salt
- 1/4 teaspoon black pepper

Directions:

1. Preheat a grill to medium-high heat. Season the salmon fillets with salt and black pepper.
2. Grill the salmon for 4-5 minutes on each side, or until fully cooked.
3. In a large bowl, combine the mixed greens, avocado, cherry tomatoes, and red onion.
4. In a small bowl, whisk together the olive oil, lemon juice, Dijon mustard, salt, and black pepper. Drizzle over the salad and toss to coat.
5. Top the salad with the grilled salmon. Serve immediately.

Nutritional Information: 350 calories, 30g protein, 10g carbohydrates, 20g fat, 4g fiber, 70mg cholesterol, 400mg sodium, 600mg potassium.

100.   Beef and Vegetable Kabobs

Yield: 4 servings | Prep time: 20 minutes | Cook time: 10 minutes

Ingredients:

- 1 pound beef sirloin, cut into 1-inch cubes
- 1 red bell pepper, cut into 1-inch pieces
- 1 green bell pepper, cut into 1-inch pieces
- 1 red onion, cut into 1-inch pieces
- 1 zucchini, cut into 1-inch pieces
- 1/4 cup olive oil

- 2 tablespoons soy sauce (low-sodium)
- 1 tablespoon Worcestershire sauce
- 2 cloves garlic, minced
- 1 teaspoon dried oregano
- 1/4 teaspoon salt
- 1/4 teaspoon black pepper

Directions:

1. In a large bowl, combine the olive oil, soy sauce, Worcestershire sauce, minced garlic, dried oregano, salt, and black pepper. Add the beef cubes and vegetables, tossing to coat. Marinate for at least 30 minutes.
2. Preheat a grill to medium-high heat. Thread the beef and vegetables onto skewers, alternating between them.
3. Grill the kabobs for 8-10 minutes, turning occasionally, until the beef is cooked to your desired doneness and the vegetables are tender.
4. Serve immediately.

Nutritional Information: 300 calories, 25g protein, 10g carbohydrates, 18g fat, 2g fiber, 70mg cholesterol, 600mg sodium, 600mg potassium.

101.   Turkey Meatloaf with Cauliflower Mash

Yield: 4 servings | Prep time: 15 minutes | Cook time: 45 minutes

Ingredients:

- 1 pound ground turkey
- 1/2 cup whole wheat breadcrumbs
- 1/4 cup grated Parmesan cheese
- 1 egg, beaten
- 1/4 cup onion, finely chopped
- 2 cloves garlic, minced
- 1/4 cup ketchup
- 1 tablespoon Worcestershire sauce
- 1 teaspoon dried thyme
- 1/4 teaspoon salt
- 1/4 teaspoon black pepper

Cauliflower Mash:

- 1 large head cauliflower, cut into florets
- 1/4 cup milk
- 2 tablespoons butter
- 1/4 teaspoon salt
- 1/4 teaspoon black pepper

Directions:

1. Preheat the oven to 375°F (190°C). In a large bowl, combine the ground turkey, breadcrumbs, grated Parmesan cheese, beaten egg, onion, garlic, ketchup, Worcestershire sauce, dried thyme, salt, and black pepper. Mix until well combined.
2. Shape the mixture into a loaf and place it in a baking dish. Bake for 45 minutes, or until fully cooked.
3. While the meatloaf is baking, steam the cauliflower florets until tender, about 10 minutes.
4. In a food processor, combine the steamed cauliflower, milk, butter, salt, and black pepper. Process until smooth.
5. Serve the turkey meatloaf with cauliflower mash on the side.

Nutritional Information: 350 calories, 25g protein, 20g carbohydrates, 18g fat, 5g fiber, 100mg cholesterol, 600mg sodium, 700mg potassium.

102.   Stuffed Cabbage Rolls

Yield: 4 servings | Prep time: 20 minutes | Cook time: 60 minutes

Ingredients:
- 1 head green cabbage
- 1 pound ground beef
- 1/2 cup cooked rice
- 1 onion, finely chopped
- 2 cloves garlic, minced
- 1 egg, beaten
- 1 teaspoon dried thyme
- 1/4 teaspoon salt
- 1/4 teaspoon black pepper
- 2 cups tomato sauce
- 1 tablespoon olive oil

Directions:

1. Preheat the oven to 350°F (175°C). Bring a large pot of water to a boil. Remove the core from the cabbage and carefully separate the leaves. Blanch the leaves in boiling water for 2-3 minutes until pliable. Drain and set aside.
2. In a large bowl, combine the ground beef, cooked rice, onion, garlic, beaten egg, dried thyme, salt, and black pepper. Mix until well combined.
3. Place about 1/4 cup of the beef mixture in the center of each cabbage leaf. Fold in the sides and roll up tightly.
4. In a large skillet, heat the olive oil over medium heat. Add the cabbage rolls seam-side down and cook for 2-3 minutes until browned.
5. Transfer the cabbage rolls to a baking dish and pour the tomato sauce over them. Cover with aluminum foil and bake for 45-60 minutes, or until fully cooked. Serve warm.

Nutritional Information: 350 calories, 25g protein, 20g carbohydrates, 18g fat, 6g fiber, 100mg cholesterol, 600mg sodium, 700mg potassium.

103.   Roasted Turkey Breast with Brussels Sprouts

Yield: 4 servings | Prep time: 15 minutes | Cook time: 60 minutes

Ingredients:
- 1 turkey breast (2 pounds)
- 1 pound Brussels sprouts, halved
- 2 tablespoons olive oil
- 1 tablespoon fresh rosemary, chopped
- 1 tablespoon fresh thyme, chopped
- 2 cloves garlic, minced
- 1 lemon, zested and juiced
- 1/4 teaspoon salt
- 1/4 teaspoon black pepper

Directions:
1. Preheat the oven to 375°F (190°C). Place the turkey breast in a roasting pan.
2. In a small bowl, mix the olive oil, fresh rosemary, fresh thyme, minced garlic, lemon zest, salt, and black pepper. Rub the mixture all over the turkey breast.
3. Arrange the Brussels sprouts around the turkey in the roasting pan. Drizzle with olive oil and season with salt and black pepper.
4. Roast for 50-60 minutes, or until the turkey reaches an internal temperature of 165°F (75°C) and the Brussels sprouts are tender and caramelized. Let the turkey rest for 10 minutes before slicing. Serve with a squeeze of lemon juice.

Nutritional Information: 350 calories, 35g protein, 12g carbohydrates, 18g fat, 4g fiber, 100mg cholesterol, 400mg sodium, 700mg potassium.

104.   Zucchini and Ground Beef Skillet

Yield: 4 servings | Prep time: 10 minutes | Cook time: 20 minutes

Ingredients:

- 1 pound ground beef
- 2 zucchinis, diced
- 1 onion, diced
- 2 cloves garlic, minced
- 1 can (14.5 oz) diced tomatoes
- 1 teaspoon dried oregano

- 1 teaspoon dried basil
- 1/4 teaspoon salt
- 1/4 teaspoon black pepper
- 1/4 cup grated Parmesan cheese
- 2 tablespoons olive oil

Directions:

1. In a large skillet, heat the olive oil over medium-high heat. Add the ground beef, onion, salt, and black pepper. Cook until the beef is no longer pink, about 5-7 minutes.
2. Add the garlic and cook for another 1-2 minutes until fragrant.
3. Stir in the diced zucchinis, diced tomatoes, dried oregano, and dried basil. Cook for 10-12 minutes until the zucchinis are tender.
4. Sprinkle with grated Parmesan cheese before serving. Serve warm.

Nutritional Information: 350 calories, 25g protein, 12g carbohydrates, 24g fat, 3g fiber, 80mg cholesterol, 600mg sodium, 700mg potassium.

105.   Roasted Lemon Herb Chicken

Yield: 4 servings | Prep time: 10 minutes | Cook time: 50 minutes

Ingredients:

- 1 whole chicken (about 4 pounds)
- 1/4 cup olive oil
- 4 cloves garlic, minced
- 1 tablespoon fresh rosemary, chopped

- 1 tablespoon fresh thyme, chopped
- 1 lemon, sliced
- 1/4 teaspoon salt
- 1/4 teaspoon black pepper

Directions:

1. Preheat the oven to 375°F (190°C). Place the chicken in a roasting pan.
2. In a small bowl, combine the olive oil, minced garlic, fresh rosemary, fresh thyme, salt, and black pepper.
3. Rub the herb mixture all over the chicken, including under the skin. Arrange the lemon slices around the chicken.
4. Roast for 45-50 minutes, or until the chicken reaches an internal temperature of 165°F (75°C). Let the chicken rest for 10 minutes before carving. Serve warm.

Nutritional Information: 450 calories, 35g protein, 1g carbohydrates, 34g fat, 0g fiber, 120mg cholesterol, 400mg sodium, 400mg potassium.

106.   Broiled Swordfish with Citrus Salsa

Yield: 4 servings | Prep time: 10 minutes | Cook time: 10 minutes

Ingredients:

- 4 swordfish steaks (6 oz each)
- 1/4 cup olive oil
- 1 teaspoon lemon zest
- 1 teaspoon lime zest
- 1/4 teaspoon salt
- 1/4 teaspoon black pepper

Citrus Salsa:

- 1 orange, peeled and diced
- 1 grapefruit, peeled and diced
- 1 lime, juiced
- 1/4 cup red onion, finely chopped
- 1/4 cup fresh cilantro, chopped
- 1 jalapeño, seeded and minced
- 1 tablespoon olive oil
- 1/4 teaspoon salt
- 1/4 teaspoon black pepper

Directions:

1. Preheat the broiler. Brush the swordfish steaks with olive oil and season with lemon zest, lime zest, salt, and black pepper.
2. Broil the swordfish steaks for 4-5 minutes on each side, or until the fish is opaque and flakes easily with a fork.
3. While the fish is broiling, prepare the citrus salsa. In a medium bowl, combine the diced orange, diced grapefruit, lime juice, red onion, fresh cilantro, jalapeño, olive oil, salt, and black pepper. Mix well.
4. Serve the broiled swordfish topped with citrus salsa. Serve immediately.

Nutritional Information: 350 calories, 30g protein, 15g carbohydrates, 20g fat, 4g fiber, 70mg cholesterol, 400mg sodium, 800mg potassium.

107. Baked Eggplant with Tomato Sauce

Yield: 4 servings | Prep time: 15 minutes | Cook time: 30 minutes

Ingredients:

- 2 large eggplants, sliced into rounds
- 2 cups marinara sauce
- 1 cup shredded mozzarella cheese
- 1/2 cup grated Parmesan cheese
- 1/4 cup fresh basil, chopped
- 1/4 cup olive oil
- 1/4 teaspoon salt
- 1/4 teaspoon black pepper

Directions:

1. Preheat the oven to 375°F (190°C). Line a baking sheet with parchment paper.
2. Arrange the eggplant slices on the prepared baking sheet. Drizzle with olive oil and season with salt and black pepper. Bake for 20 minutes, or until tender and golden brown.
3. In a baking dish, spread a thin layer of marinara sauce. Layer the baked eggplant slices, marinara sauce, shredded mozzarella cheese, and grated Parmesan cheese. Repeat the layers until all the ingredients are used, ending with a layer of cheese.
4. Bake for an additional 10 minutes, or until the cheese is melted and bubbly. Garnish with fresh basil. Serve warm.

Nutritional Information: 300 calories, 12g protein, 20g carbohydrates, 20g fat, 6g fiber, 30mg cholesterol, 600mg sodium, 700mg potassium.

108. Shrimp Scampi with Zucchini Noodles

Yield: 4 servings | Prep time: 10 minutes | Cook time: 10 minutes

Ingredients:

- 1 pound large shrimp, peeled and deveined
- 4 medium zucchinis, spiralized
- 3 cloves garlic, minced
- 1/4 cup white wine (optional)
- 1/4 cup chicken broth
- 2 tablespoons lemon juice
- 1 tablespoon olive oil
- 1/4 teaspoon red pepper flakes
- 1/4 teaspoon salt
- 1/4 teaspoon black pepper
- 1/4 cup fresh parsley, chopped

Directions:

1. In a large skillet, heat the olive oil over medium-high heat. Add the garlic and cook for 1-2 minutes until fragrant.
2. Add the shrimp, red pepper flakes, salt, and black pepper. Cook for 2-3 minutes on each side, or until the shrimp are pink and opaque. Remove the shrimp from the skillet and set aside.
3. In the same skillet, add the white wine (if using), chicken broth, and lemon juice. Bring to a simmer and cook for 2-3 minutes.
4. Add the zucchini noodles to the skillet and cook for 2-3 minutes until just tender.
5. Return the shrimp to the skillet and toss to combine with the zoodles. Garnish with fresh parsley. Serve immediately.

Nutritional Information: 250 calories, 25g protein, 10g carbohydrates, 10g fat, 4g fiber, 170mg cholesterol, 600mg sodium, 700mg potassium.

109. Thai Peanut Chicken with Veggie Noodles

Yield: 4 servings | Prep time: 15 minutes | Cook time: 15 minutes

Ingredients:

- 2 boneless, skinless chicken breasts, thinly sliced
- 2 medium zucchinis, spiralized
- 2 medium carrots, spiralized
- 1 red bell pepper, sliced
- 1/2 cup peanut butter
- 1/4 cup soy sauce (low-sodium)
- 2 tablespoons lime juice
- 2 tablespoons honey
- 2 cloves garlic, minced
- 1 tablespoon fresh ginger, grated
- 1/4 teaspoon red pepper flakes (optional)
- 1 tablespoon olive oil
- 1/4 cup chopped peanuts
- 1/4 cup fresh cilantro, chopped

Directions:

1. In a small bowl, whisk together the peanut butter, soy sauce, lime juice, honey, minced garlic, fresh ginger, and red pepper flakes (if using). Set aside.
2. In a large skillet, heat the olive oil over medium-high heat. Add the sliced chicken and cook for 5-7 minutes until fully cooked.
3. Add the spiralized zucchinis, carrots, and red bell pepper to the skillet. Cook for another 3-4 minutes until the vegetables are tender-crisp.
4. Pour the peanut sauce over the chicken and vegetables. Toss to coat and cook for an additional 1-2 minutes until heated through.
5. Serve the Thai peanut chicken topped with chopped peanuts and fresh cilantro.

Nutritional Information: 400 calories, 30g protein, 20g carbohydrates, 22g fat, 4g fiber, 60mg cholesterol, 800mg sodium, 600mg potassium.

110.   Garlic Butter Shrimp and Veggie Foil Packets

Yield: 4 servings | Prep time: 10 minutes | Cook time: 15 minutes

Ingredients:

- 1 pound large shrimp, peeled and deveined
- 2 zucchinis, sliced
- 1 red bell pepper, sliced
- 1 yellow bell pepper, sliced
- 1/4 cup butter, melted
- 4 cloves garlic, minced
- 1 tablespoon fresh parsley, chopped
- 1 lemon, sliced
- 1/4 teaspoon salt
- 1/4 teaspoon black pepper

Directions:

1. Preheat the grill to medium-high heat. In a large bowl, combine the melted butter, minced garlic, fresh parsley, salt, and black pepper.
2. Add the shrimp, zucchinis, and bell peppers to the bowl and toss to coat.
3. Divide the shrimp and vegetable mixture among four large pieces of aluminum foil. Top with lemon slices.
4. Fold the foil over the shrimp and vegetables to create packets. Grill for 10-12 minutes, or until the shrimp are pink and opaque and the vegetables are tender.
5. Serve the foil packets immediately.

Nutritional Information: 300 calories, 25g protein, 10g carbohydrates, 18g fat, 2g fiber, 170mg cholesterol, 600mg sodium, 700mg potassium.

111.   Turkey Sausage and Peppers

Yield: 4 servings | Prep time: 10 minutes | Cook time: 20 minutes

Ingredients:

- 1 pound turkey sausage, sliced
- 2 red bell peppers, sliced
- 2 yellow bell peppers, sliced
- 1 onion, sliced
- 2 cloves garlic, minced
- 1 tablespoon olive oil
- 1 teaspoon dried oregano
- 1 teaspoon dried basil
- 1/4 teaspoon salt
- 1/4 teaspoon black pepper

Directions:

1. In a large skillet, heat the olive oil over medium-high heat. Add the sliced turkey sausage and cook for 5-7 minutes until browned.
2. Add the sliced bell peppers, onion, and garlic to the skillet. Cook for another 7-10 minutes until the vegetables are tender.
3. Stir in the dried oregano, dried basil, salt, and black pepper. Cook for an additional 1-2 minutes until heated through.
4. Serve immediately.

Nutritional Information: 320 calories, 25g protein, 12g carbohydrates, 18g fat, 4g fiber, 80mg cholesterol, 600mg sodium, 700mg potassium.

112. Spinach and Ricotta Stuffed Chicken

Yield: 4 servings | Prep time: 15 minutes | Cook time: 30 minutes

Ingredients:

- 4 boneless, skinless chicken breasts
- 1 cup fresh spinach, chopped
- 1/2 cup ricotta cheese
- 1/4 cup grated Parmesan cheese

- 2 cloves garlic, minced
- 1 tablespoon olive oil
- 1/4 teaspoon salt
- 1/4 teaspoon black pepper

Directions:

1. Preheat the oven to 375°F (190°C). Slice each chicken breast horizontally to create a pocket.
2. In a medium bowl, combine the chopped spinach, ricotta cheese, grated Parmesan cheese, minced garlic, salt, and black pepper. Mix well.
3. Stuff each chicken breast with the spinach and ricotta mixture. Secure with toothpicks if necessary.
4. Heat the olive oil in a large skillet over medium-high heat. Sear the chicken breasts for 2-3 minutes on each side until golden brown.
5. Transfer the seared chicken breasts to a baking dish and bake for 20-25 minutes, or until the chicken is fully cooked. Serve warm.

Nutritional Information: 320 calories, 35g protein, 6g carbohydrates, 18g fat, 1g fiber, 90mg cholesterol, 450mg sodium, 600mg potassium.

113. Moroccan Spiced Lamb Chops

Yield: 4 servings | Prep time: 10 minutes | Cook time: 15 minutes

Ingredients:

- 8 lamb chops
- 2 tablespoons olive oil
- 1 tablespoon ground cumin
- 1 tablespoon ground coriander
- 1 teaspoon ground cinnamon
- 1 teaspoon ground paprika

- 1/2 teaspoon ground turmeric
- 1/4 teaspoon salt
- 1/4 teaspoon black pepper
- 1/4 cup fresh mint leaves, chopped (optional)

Directions:

1. In a small bowl, combine the olive oil, ground cumin, ground coriander, ground cinnamon, ground paprika, ground turmeric, salt, and black pepper to create a marinade.
2. Rub the marinade all over the lamb chops and let sit for at least 30 minutes.
3. Preheat a grill to medium-high heat. Grill the lamb chops for 3-4 minutes on each side, or until they reach your desired level of doneness.
4. Garnish with fresh mint leaves if desired. Serve immediately.

Nutritional Information: 350 calories, 30g protein, 2g carbohydrates, 24g fat, 1g fiber, 90mg cholesterol, 400mg sodium, 400mg potassium.

114. Quinoa and Vegetable Stuffed Peppers

Yield: 4 servings | Prep time: 15 minutes | Cook time: 25 minutes

Ingredients:

- 4 large bell peppers
- 1 cup cooked quinoa
- 1 cup black beans, rinsed and drained
- 1 cup corn kernels
- 1 cup diced tomatoes

- 1/2 cup shredded cheddar cheese
- 1 teaspoon ground cumin
- 1/2 teaspoon salt
- 1/4 teaspoon black pepper
- 1/4 cup chopped fresh cilantro (optional)

Directions:

1. Preheat the oven to 375°F (190°C). Cut the tops off the bell peppers and remove the seeds.
2. In a large bowl, combine the cooked quinoa, black beans, corn, diced tomatoes, ground cumin, salt, and black pepper.
3. Stuff the bell peppers with the quinoa mixture and place them in a baking dish.
4. Cover with aluminum foil and bake for 20 minutes. Remove the foil, sprinkle the tops with shredded cheddar cheese, and bake for an additional 5 minutes, or until the cheese is melted. Garnish with chopped cilantro if desired. Serve warm.

Nutritional Information: 300 calories, 12g protein, 45g carbohydrates, 8g fat, 10g fiber, 15mg cholesterol, 450mg sodium, 800mg potassium.

115. Garlic Roasted Pork Tenderloin

Yield: 4 servings | Prep time: 10 minutes | Cook time: 25 minutes

Ingredients:

- 1 pork tenderloin (about 1 pound)
- 2 tablespoons olive oil
- 4 cloves garlic, minced
- 1 tablespoon fresh rosemary, chopped

- 1 tablespoon fresh thyme, chopped
- 1 teaspoon Dijon mustard
- 1/4 teaspoon salt
- 1/4 teaspoon black pepper

Directions:

1. Preheat the oven to 400°F (200°C). In a small bowl, combine the olive oil, minced garlic, fresh rosemary, fresh thyme, Dijon mustard, salt, and black pepper.
2. Rub the herb mixture all over the pork tenderloin.
3. Place the pork tenderloin on a baking sheet and roast for 25-30 minutes, or until the internal temperature reaches 145°F (63°C).
4. Let the pork rest for 10 minutes before slicing. Serve warm.

Nutritional Information: 280 calories, 30g protein, 2g carbohydrates, 16g fat, 0g fiber, 80mg cholesterol, 400mg sodium, 600mg potassium.

116.　Lemon Dill Salmon

Yield: 4 servings | Prep time: 10 minutes | Cook time: 15 minutes

Ingredients:

- 4 salmon fillets (4 oz each)
- 2 tablespoons olive oil
- 1 lemon, sliced
- 1 tablespoon fresh dill, chopped

- 1 teaspoon lemon zest
- 1/4 teaspoon salt
- 1/4 teaspoon black pepper

Directions:

1. Preheat the oven to 400°F (200°C). Place the salmon fillets on a baking sheet lined with parchment paper.
2. Drizzle the salmon with olive oil and season with lemon zest, salt, and black pepper.
3. Place the lemon slices on top of the salmon fillets.
4. Bake for 12-15 minutes, or until the salmon is opaque and flakes easily with a fork. Garnish with fresh dill. Serve warm.

Nutritional Information: 300 calories, 30g protein, 2g carbohydrates, 20g fat, 0g fiber, 70mg cholesterol, 400mg sodium, 600mg potassium.

117.　Cauliflower Fried Rice with Chicken

Yield: 4 servings | Prep time: 10 minutes | Cook time: 15 minutes

Ingredients:

- 2 boneless, skinless chicken breasts, diced
- 4 cups cauliflower rice
- 1 cup frozen peas and carrots
- 1/2 cup diced onion
- 2 cloves garlic, minced
- 2 eggs, beaten

- 2 tablespoons soy sauce (low-sodium)
- 1 tablespoon sesame oil
- 1/4 teaspoon salt
- 1/4 teaspoon black pepper
- 1/4 cup chopped green onions (optional)

Directions:

1. In a large skillet or wok, heat the sesame oil over medium-high heat. Add the diced chicken, salt, and black pepper. Cook until the chicken is no longer pink, about 5-7 minutes. Remove from the skillet and set aside.
2. In the same skillet, add the onion and garlic. Cook for 2-3 minutes until softened.
3. Add the cauliflower rice, frozen peas and carrots, and soy sauce. Cook for 5-7 minutes until the vegetables are tender.
4. Push the cauliflower rice mixture to one side of the skillet and add the beaten eggs. Scramble the eggs until fully cooked, then mix them into the cauliflower rice.
5. Return the chicken to the skillet and toss to combine. Garnish with chopped green onions if desired. Serve hot.

Nutritional Information: 350 calories, 30g protein, 15g carbohydrates, 20g fat, 5g fiber, 80mg cholesterol, 600mg sodium, 600mg potassium.

118. Spicy Grilled Shrimp Skewers

Yield: 4 servings | Prep time: 10 minutes | Cook time: 10 minutes

Ingredients:

- 1 pound large shrimp, peeled and deveined
- 2 tablespoons olive oil
- 1 tablespoon lime juice
- 2 cloves garlic, minced
- 1 teaspoon chili powder
- 1/2 teaspoon paprika
- 1/4 teaspoon salt
- 1/4 teaspoon black pepper
- Lime wedges for serving

Directions:

1. In a large bowl, combine the olive oil, lime juice, minced garlic, chili powder, paprika, salt, and black pepper. Add the shrimp and toss to coat. Marinate for at least 15 minutes.
2. Preheat a grill to medium-high heat. Thread the shrimp onto skewers.
3. Grill the shrimp for 2-3 minutes on each side, or until pink and opaque.
4. Serve the shrimp skewers with lime wedges.

Nutritional Information: 250 calories, 25g protein, 5g carbohydrates, 14g fat, 0g fiber, 170mg cholesterol, 600mg sodium, 700mg potassium.

119. Vegetable and Lentil Stew

Yield: 6 servings | Prep time: 10 minutes | Cook time: 30 minutes

Ingredients:

- 1 tablespoon olive oil
- 1 onion, diced
- 2 carrots, diced
- 2 celery stalks, diced
- 3 cloves garlic, minced
- 1 cup dried lentils, rinsed
- 1 can (14.5 oz) diced tomatoes
- 4 cups vegetable broth
- 1 teaspoon ground cumin
- 1/2 teaspoon dried thyme
- 1/4 teaspoon salt
- 1/4 teaspoon black pepper
- 1/4 cup fresh parsley, chopped (optional)

Directions:

1. Heat the olive oil in a large pot over medium heat. Add the onion, carrots, and celery. Sauté for 5-7 minutes until softened.
2. Add the garlic and cook for another 1-2 minutes until fragrant.
3. Stir in the lentils, diced tomatoes, vegetable broth, ground cumin, dried thyme, salt, and black pepper. Bring to a boil, then reduce heat and simmer for 25-30 minutes, or until the lentils are tender.
4. Stir in the fresh parsley (if using) and serve hot.

Nutritional Information: 250 calories, 12g protein, 38g carbohydrates, 6g fat, 12g fiber, 0mg cholesterol, 600mg sodium, 700mg potassium.

Nutritious Salads for Diabetics

120.   Cucumber and Avocado Salad

Yield: 4 servings | Prep time: 10 minutes | Cook time: 0 minutes

Ingredients:

- 2 large cucumbers, diced
- 1 avocado, diced
- 1/4 cup red onion, finely chopped
- 1/4 cup fresh cilantro, chopped

- 2 tablespoons lime juice
- 1 tablespoon olive oil
- 1/4 teaspoon salt
- 1/4 teaspoon black pepper

Directions:

1. In a large bowl, combine cucumber, avocado, red onion, and cilantro.
2. In a small bowl, whisk together lime juice, olive oil, salt, and black pepper.
3. Pour the dressing over the salad and toss gently to coat. Serve immediately.

Nutritional Information: 150 calories, 2g protein, 12g carbohydrates, 11g fat, 6g fiber, 0mg cholesterol, 200mg sodium, 450mg potassium.

121.   Greek Salad with Feta

Yield: 4 servings | Prep time: 10 minutes | Cook time: 0 minutes

Ingredients:

- 4 cups chopped romaine lettuce
- 1 cup cherry tomatoes, halved
- 1 cucumber, sliced
- 1/2 red onion, thinly sliced
- 1/2 cup Kalamata olives, pitted
- 1/4 cup crumbled feta cheese

- 2 tablespoons olive oil
- 1 tablespoon red wine vinegar
- 1 teaspoon dried oregano
- 1/4 teaspoon salt
- 1/4 teaspoon black pepper

Directions:

1. In a large bowl, combine the romaine lettuce, cherry tomatoes, cucumber, red onion, Kalamata olives, and crumbled feta cheese.
2. In a small bowl, whisk together the olive oil, red wine vinegar, dried oregano, salt, and black pepper. Drizzle over the salad and toss to coat. Serve immediately.

Nutritional Information: 200 calories, 5g protein, 10g carbohydrates, 18g fat, 3g fiber, 15mg cholesterol, 400mg sodium, 500mg potassium.

122.   Spinach and Strawberry Salad

Yield: 4 servings | Prep time: 10 minutes | Cook time: 0 minutes

Ingredients:

- 6 cups fresh spinach leaves
- 1 cup sliced strawberries
- 1/4 cup sliced almonds
- 1/4 cup crumbled goat cheese
- 2 tablespoons balsamic vinegar
- 2 tablespoons olive oil
- 1 teaspoon honey
- 1/4 teaspoon salt
- 1/4 teaspoon black pepper

Directions:

1. In a large bowl, combine the spinach leaves, sliced strawberries, sliced almonds, and crumbled goat cheese.
2. In a small bowl, whisk together the balsamic vinegar, olive oil, honey, salt, and black pepper. Drizzle over the salad and toss to coat. Serve immediately.

Nutritional Information: 180 calories, 5g protein, 15g carbohydrates, 12g fat, 3g fiber, 10mg cholesterol, 200mg sodium, 400mg potassium.

123.   Caesar Salad with Grilled Shrimp

Yield: 4 servings | Prep time: 10 minutes | Cook time: 10 minutes

Ingredients:

- 1 pound large shrimp, peeled and deveined
- 8 cups romaine lettuce, chopped
- 1/4 cup grated Parmesan cheese
- 1/2 cup croutons
- 1/4 cup Caesar dressing
- 1 tablespoon olive oil
- 1/4 teaspoon salt
- 1/4 teaspoon black pepper

Directions:

1. Preheat a grill to medium-high heat. Toss the shrimp with olive oil, salt, and black pepper.
2. Grill the shrimp for 2-3 minutes on each side, or until pink and opaque.
3. In a large bowl, combine the chopped romaine lettuce, grated Parmesan cheese, and croutons.
4. Drizzle with Caesar dressing and toss to coat.
5. Top the salad with the grilled shrimp. Serve immediately.

Nutritional Information: 250 calories, 20g protein, 12g carbohydrates, 14g fat, 3g fiber, 150mg cholesterol, 500mg sodium, 400mg potassium.

124.　　Arugula and Walnut Salad

Yield: 4 servings | Prep time: 10 minutes | Cook time: 0 minutes

Ingredients:

- 4 cups arugula
- 1/2 cup walnut halves
- 1/4 cup crumbled goat cheese
- 1 apple, thinly sliced
- 2 tablespoons olive oil

- 1 tablespoon balsamic vinegar
- 1 teaspoon Dijon mustard
- 1/4 teaspoon salt
- 1/4 teaspoon black pepper

Directions:

1. In a large bowl, combine arugula, walnuts, goat cheese, and apple slices.
2. In a small bowl, whisk together olive oil, balsamic vinegar, Dijon mustard, salt, and black pepper.
3. Drizzle the dressing over the salad and toss to coat. Serve immediately.

Nutritional Information: 200 calories, 5g protein, 10g carbohydrates, 16g fat, 3g fiber, 5mg cholesterol, 200mg sodium, 300mg potassium.

125.　　Caprese Salad

Yield: 4 servings | Prep time: 10 minutes | Cook time: 0 minutes

Ingredients:

- 4 large tomatoes, sliced
- 1 pound fresh mozzarella, sliced
- 1/4 cup fresh basil leaves
- 2 tablespoons balsamic glaze
- 2 tablespoons olive oil
- 1/4 teaspoon salt
- 1/4 teaspoon black pepper

Directions:

1. On a serving platter, arrange the tomato slices and mozzarella slices in an alternating pattern.
2. Tuck the fresh basil leaves between the tomato and mozzarella slices.
3. Drizzle with balsamic glaze and olive oil. Sprinkle with salt and black pepper. Serve immediately.

Nutritional Information: 250 calories, 16g protein, 10g carbohydrates, 18g fat, 2g fiber, 50mg cholesterol, 400mg sodium, 400mg potassium.

126.   Tuna Salad with Avocado

Yield: 4 servings | Prep time: 10 minutes | Cook time: 0 minutes

Ingredients:

- 2 cans (5 oz each) tuna, drained
- 1 avocado, diced
- 1/4 cup diced red onion
- 1/4 cup diced celery

- 1/4 cup mayonnaise
- 1 tablespoon lemon juice
- 1/4 teaspoon salt
- 1/4 teaspoon black pepper

Directions:

1. In a large bowl, combine the tuna, diced avocado, red onion, celery, mayonnaise, lemon juice, salt, and black pepper. Mix well.
2. Serve immediately or refrigerate until ready to serve.

Nutritional Information: 250 calories, 20g protein, 8g carbohydrates, 16g fat, 4g fiber, 40mg cholesterol, 400mg sodium, 500mg potassium.

127.   Asian Chicken Salad

Yield: 4 servings | Prep time: 15 minutes | Cook time: 10 minutes

Ingredients:

- 2 boneless, skinless chicken breasts
- 4 cups shredded cabbage
- 1 cup shredded carrots
- 1/2 cup sliced bell peppers
- 1/4 cup sliced almonds
- 1/4 cup chopped green onions
- 2 tablespoons soy sauce (low-sodium)

- 2 tablespoons rice vinegar
- 1 tablespoon sesame oil
- 1 tablespoon honey
- 1 teaspoon grated ginger
- 1 clove garlic, minced
- 1/4 teaspoon salt
- 1/4 teaspoon black pepper

Directions:

1. Preheat a grill to medium-high heat. Season the chicken breasts with salt and black pepper.
2. Grill the chicken for 5-7 minutes on each side, or until fully cooked. Let cool and slice.
3. In a large bowl, combine the shredded cabbage, shredded carrots, sliced bell peppers, sliced almonds, and chopped green onions.
4. In a small bowl, whisk together the soy sauce, rice vinegar, sesame oil, honey, grated ginger, and minced garlic. Drizzle over the salad and toss to coat.
5. Top the salad with the grilled chicken slices. Serve immediately.

Nutritional Information: 300 calories, 25g protein, 15g carbohydrates, 16g fat, 4g fiber, 70mg cholesterol, 600mg sodium, 500mg potassium.

128.   Roasted Beet and Goat Cheese Salad

Yield: 4 servings | Prep time: 10 minutes | Cook time: 40 minutes

Ingredients:

- 4 medium beets, peeled and diced
- 6 cups mixed greens
- 1/4 cup crumbled goat cheese
- 1/4 cup walnuts, chopped
- 2 tablespoons balsamic vinegar
- 2 tablespoons olive oil
- 1 teaspoon honey
- 1/4 teaspoon salt
- 1/4 teaspoon black pepper

Directions:

1. Preheat the oven to 400°F (200°C). Line a baking sheet with parchment paper.
2. Place the diced beets on the prepared baking sheet and drizzle with olive oil. Sprinkle with salt and black pepper. Roast for 30-40 minutes, or until tender and slightly caramelized.
3. In a large bowl, combine the mixed greens, roasted beets, crumbled goat cheese, and chopped walnuts.
4. In a small bowl, whisk together the balsamic vinegar, olive oil, honey, salt, and black pepper. Drizzle over the salad and toss to coat. Serve immediately.

Nutritional Information: 250 calories, 8g protein, 20g carbohydrates, 16g fat, 5g fiber, 10mg cholesterol, 400mg sodium, 600mg potassium.

129.   Tomato and Mozzarella Salad

Yield: 4 servings | Prep time: 10 minutes | Cook time: 0 minutes

Ingredients:

- 4 large tomatoes, sliced
- 1 pound fresh mozzarella, sliced
- 1/4 cup fresh basil leaves
- 2 tablespoons balsamic glaze
- 2 tablespoons olive oil
- 1/4 teaspoon salt
- 1/4 teaspoon black pepper

Directions:

1. On a serving platter, arrange the tomato slices and mozzarella slices in an alternating pattern.
2. Tuck the fresh basil leaves between the tomato and mozzarella slices.
3. Drizzle with balsamic glaze and olive oil. Sprinkle with salt and black pepper. Serve immediately.

Nutritional Information: 250 calories, 16g protein, 10g carbohydrates, 18g fat, 2g fiber, 50mg cholesterol, 400mg sodium, 400mg potassium.

130. Southwest Chicken Salad

Yield: 4 servings | Prep time: 15 minutes | Cook time: 10 minutes

Ingredients:

- 2 boneless, skinless chicken breasts
- 6 cups romaine lettuce, chopped
- 1 cup corn kernels
- 1 cup black beans, rinsed and drained
- 1/2 cup diced red bell pepper
- 1/4 cup diced red onion
- 1/4 cup shredded cheddar cheese
- 1/4 cup salsa
- 1/4 cup sour cream
- 1 tablespoon olive oil
- 1 teaspoon ground cumin
- 1/4 teaspoon salt
- 1/4 teaspoon black pepper

Directions:

1. Preheat a grill to medium-high heat. Season the chicken breasts with ground cumin, salt, and black pepper.
2. Grill the chicken for 5-7 minutes on each side, or until fully cooked. Let cool and slice.
3. In a large bowl, combine the romaine lettuce, corn kernels, black beans, diced red bell pepper, diced red onion, shredded cheddar cheese, salsa, and sour cream. Toss to combine.
4. Top the salad with the grilled chicken slices. Serve immediately.

Nutritional Information: 350 calories, 30g protein, 25g carbohydrates, 14g fat, 6g fiber, 80mg cholesterol, 600mg sodium, 500mg potassium.

131. Spinach and Bacon Salad

Yield: 4 servings | Prep time: 10 minutes | Cook time: 10 minutes

Ingredients:

- 6 cups fresh spinach leaves
- 4 slices bacon, cooked and crumbled
- 1/4 cup red onion, thinly sliced
- 1/4 cup sliced mushrooms
- 2 hard-boiled eggs, sliced
- 2 tablespoons red wine vinegar
- 2 tablespoons olive oil
- 1 teaspoon Dijon mustard
- 1/4 teaspoon salt
- 1/4 teaspoon black pepper

Directions:

1. In a large bowl, combine the spinach leaves, crumbled bacon, sliced red onion, and sliced mushrooms.
2. In a small bowl, whisk together the red wine vinegar, olive oil, Dijon mustard, salt, and black pepper. Drizzle over the salad and toss to coat.
3. Top the salad with sliced hard-boiled eggs. Serve immediately.

Nutritional Information: 250 calories, 12g protein, 6g carbohydrates, 20g fat, 3g fiber, 210mg cholesterol, 400mg sodium, 500mg potassium.

132.   Chickpea and Cucumber Salad

Yield: 4 servings | Prep time: 10 minutes | Cook time: 0 minutes

Ingredients:

- 2 cans (15 oz each) chickpeas, rinsed and drained
- 1 cucumber, diced
- 1/2 red onion, finely chopped
- 1/4 cup fresh parsley, chopped

- 1/4 cup olive oil
- 2 tablespoons lemon juice
- 1 teaspoon lemon zest
- 1/2 teaspoon salt
- 1/4 teaspoon black pepper

Directions:

1. In a large bowl, combine the chickpeas, diced cucumber, finely chopped red onion, and fresh parsley.
2. In a small bowl, whisk together the olive oil, lemon juice, lemon zest, salt, and black pepper. Drizzle over the chickpea mixture and toss to coat. Serve immediately.

Nutritional Information: 250 calories, 8g protein, 30g carbohydrates, 12g fat, 8g fiber, 0mg cholesterol, 300mg sodium, 500mg potassium.

133.   Mediterranean Quinoa Salad

Yield: 4 servings | Prep time: 10 minutes | Cook time: 15 minutes

Ingredients:

- 1 cup quinoa
- 2 cups water
- 1 cup cherry tomatoes, halved
- 1/2 cucumber, diced
- 1/4 cup Kalamata olives, pitted and sliced
- 1/4 cup crumbled feta cheese

- 1/4 cup olive oil
- 2 tablespoons lemon juice
- 1 tablespoon red wine vinegar
- 1 teaspoon dried oregano
- 1/4 teaspoon salt
- 1/4 teaspoon black pepper

Directions:

1. Rinse the quinoa under cold water. In a medium saucepan, bring the quinoa and water to a boil.
2. Reduce the heat to low, cover, and simmer for 15 minutes, or until the quinoa is cooked and the water is absorbed. Let cool.
3. In a large bowl, combine the cooked quinoa, cherry tomatoes, cucumber, Kalamata olives, and crumbled feta cheese.
4. In a small bowl, whisk together the olive oil, lemon juice, red wine vinegar, dried oregano, salt, and black pepper. Drizzle over the salad and toss to coat. Serve immediately.

Nutritional Information: 250 calories, 8g protein, 28g carbohydrates, 12g fat, 4g fiber, 10mg cholesterol, 300mg sodium, 400mg potassium.

Healthy Snacks for Diabetics

134.   Cottage Cheese with Pineapple

Yield: 2 servings | Prep time: 5 minutes | Cook time: 0 minutes

Ingredients:

- 1 cup cottage cheese
- 1 cup pineapple chunks (fresh or canned, drained)

Directions:

1. In a bowl, combine the cottage cheese and pineapple chunks. Mix well.
2. Serve immediately.

Nutritional Information: 150 calories, 12g protein, 20g carbohydrates, 2g fat, 1g fiber, 10mg cholesterol, 300mg sodium, 200mg potassium.

135.   Hard-Boiled Eggs

Yield: 6 servings | Prep time: 5 minutes | Cook time: 10 minutes

Ingredients:

- 6 large eggs

Directions:

1. Place the eggs in a single layer in a saucepan and cover with cold water.
2. Bring to a boil over medium-high heat. Once boiling, cover the saucepan and remove from heat. Let sit for 10 minutes.
3. Drain the hot water and transfer the eggs to a bowl of ice water to cool. Peel the eggs and serve.

Nutritional Information: 70 calories, 6g protein, 1g carbohydrates, 5g fat, 0g fiber, 185mg cholesterol, 65mg sodium, 60mg potassium.

136.   Mixed Nuts

Yield: 4 servings | Prep time: 0 minutes | Cook time: 0 minutes

Ingredients:

- 1 cup mixed nuts (such as almonds, walnuts, cashews, and pecans)

Directions:

1. Serve the mixed nuts in small bowls.

Nutritional Information: 200 calories, 5g protein, 8g carbohydrates, 18g fat, 3g fiber, 0mg cholesterol, 0mg sodium, 200mg potassium.

137.   Avocado Slices with Lime and Sea Salt

Yield: 2 servings | Prep time: 5 minutes | Cook time: 0 minutes

Ingredients:

- 1 avocado, sliced
- 1/2 lime
- 1/4 teaspoon sea salt

Directions:

1. Arrange the avocado slices on a plate. Squeeze the lime over the avocado and sprinkle with sea salt. Serve immediately.

Nutritional Information: 150 calories, 2g protein, 12g carbohydrates, 12g fat, 8g fiber, 0mg cholesterol, 200mg sodium, 500mg potassium.

138.   Fresh Strawberries with Greek Yogurt Dip

Yield: 4 servings | Prep time: 5 minutes | Cook time: 0 minutes

Ingredients:

- 2 cups fresh strawberries, hulled
- 1 cup Greek yogurt
- 1 tablespoon honey
- 1/2 teaspoon vanilla extract

Directions:

1. In a medium bowl, mix the Greek yogurt, honey, and vanilla extract until well combined.
2. Serve the fresh strawberries with the Greek yogurt dip.

Nutritional Information: 100 calories, 5g protein, 18g carbohydrates, 2g fat, 2g fiber, 5mg cholesterol, 30mg sodium, 200mg potassium.

139. Berry Smoothie with Almond Milk

Yield: 2 servings | Prep time: 5 minutes | Cook time: 0 minutes

Ingredients:

- 1 cup mixed berries (such as strawberries, blueberries, and raspberries)
- 1 cup unsweetened almond milk
- 1 tablespoon honey (optional)
- 1/2 teaspoon vanilla extract

Directions:

1. In a blender, combine the mixed berries, almond milk, honey (if using), and vanilla extract. Blend until smooth.
2. Pour into glasses and serve immediately.

Nutritional Information: 100 calories, 2g protein, 20g carbohydrates, 3g fat, 5g fiber, 0mg cholesterol, 100mg sodium, 300mg potassium.

140. Cucumber Slices with Cream Cheese

Yield: 2 servings | Prep time: 5 minutes | Cook time: 0 minutes

Ingredients:

- 1 cucumber, sliced
- 1/4 cup cream cheese

Directions:

1. Spread the cream cheese on the cucumber slices. Serve immediately.

Nutritional Information: 100 calories, 2g protein, 6g carbohydrates, 8g fat, 1g fiber, 25mg cholesterol, 100mg sodium, 200mg potassium.

141. Apple Slices with Cheese

Yield: 2 servings | Prep time: 5 minutes | Cook time: 0 minutes

Ingredients:

- 1 apple, sliced
- 2 oz cheese (such as cheddar, Swiss, or Gouda)

Directions:

1. Serve the apple slices with the cheese.

Nutritional Information: 150 calories, 6g protein, 18g carbohydrates, 8g fat, 3g fiber, 20mg cholesterol, 150mg sodium, 200mg potassium.

142. Cheese and Whole Grain Crackers

Yield: 2 servings | Prep time: 5 minutes | Cook time: 0 minutes

Ingredients:

- 2 oz cheese (such as cheddar, Swiss, or Gouda)
- 12 whole grain crackers

Directions:

1. Serve the cheese with the whole grain crackers.

Nutritional Information: 200 calories, 8g protein, 18g carbohydrates, 12g fat, 2g fiber, 30mg cholesterol, 250mg sodium, 150mg potassium.

143. Edamame

Yield: 4 servings | Prep time: 5 minutes | Cook time: 5 minutes

Ingredients:

- 2 cups edamame (in the pods)
- 1/4 teaspoon sea salt

Directions:

1. Bring a pot of water to a boil. Add the edamame and cook for 3-5 minutes, or until tender.
2. Drain and sprinkle with sea salt. Serve immediately.

Nutritional Information: 120 calories, 10g protein, 12g carbohydrates, 4g fat, 4g fiber, 0mg cholesterol, 100mg sodium, 300mg potassium.

144. Turkey Roll-Ups with Lettuce

Yield: 2 servings | Prep time: 5 minutes | Cook time: 0 minutes

Ingredients:

- 4 slices deli turkey
- 4 large lettuce leaves
- 1/4 cup hummus

Directions:

1. Spread the hummus on each slice of turkey. Place a lettuce leaf on top and roll up. Serve immediately.

Nutritional Information: 150 calories, 14g protein, 8g carbohydrates, 7g fat, 2g fiber, 30mg cholesterol, 600mg sodium, 300mg potassium.

30-Day Meal Plan

This 30-day meal plan incorporates a variety of recipes from the "Balanced Breakfasts for Diabetics," "Wholesome Lunches for Diabetics," and "Delicious Dinners for Diabetics" sections to provide you with diverse and delicious meals. Each day includes a breakfast, lunch, and dinner to ensure you get a balanced diet that supports your health and diabetes management.

Day 1

- **Breakfast:** Veggie Omelet; 28
- **Lunch:** Spaghetti Squash with Marinara Sauce; 47
- **Dinner:** Baked Salmon with Asparagus; 68

Day 2

- **Breakfast:** Whole Grain English Muffin with Peanut Butter; 28
- **Lunch:** Chickpea Salad with Lemon Dressing; 47
- **Dinner:** Grilled Chicken with Steamed Vegetables; 68

Day 3

- **Breakfast:** Berry Smoothie Bowl; 29
- **Lunch:** Moroccan Lentil Stew; 48
- **Dinner:** Beef and Broccoli Stir-Fry; 69

Day 4

- **Breakfast:** Greek Yogurt Parfait with Berries; 29
- **Lunch:** Lentil and Cucumber Salad; 48
- **Dinner:** Lemon Garlic Shrimp with Zoodles; 69

Day 5

- **Breakfast:** Avocado Toast on Whole Grain Bread; 30
- **Lunch:** Vegetable and Hummus Wrap; 49
- **Dinner:** Spaghetti Squash with Turkey Meatballs; 70

Day 6

- **Breakfast:** Almond Butter and Apple Slices; 30
- **Lunch:** Zucchini Noodles with Pesto and Cherry Tomatoes; 49
- **Dinner:** Chicken Fajita Bowl; 71

Day 7

- **Breakfast:** Spinach and Feta Scramble; 31
- **Lunch:** Zucchini Noodles with Pesto; 51
- **Dinner:** Stuffed Bell Peppers with Ground Turkey; 72

Day 8

- **Breakfast:** Chia Seed Pudding with Almond Milk; 31
- **Lunch:** Quinoa and Black Bean Bowl; 51
- **Dinner:** Grilled Tuna with Mango Salsa; 72

Day 9

- **Breakfast:** Oatmeal with Flax Seeds and Fresh Berries; 32
- **Lunch:** Grilled Chicken Salad; 52
- **Dinner:** Chicken and Spinach Stuffed Portobellos; 73

Day 10

- **Breakfast:** Egg Muffins with Vegetables; 32
- **Lunch:** Chicken and Cauliflower Rice Bowl; 52
- **Dinner:** Grilled Pork Chops with Apple Slaw; 73

Day 11

- **Breakfast:** Low-Carb Breakfast Burrito; 33
- **Lunch:** Turkey and Avocado Wrap; 53
- **Dinner:** Cauliflower Crust Pizza; 74

Day 12

- **Breakfast:** Smoothie with Spinach, Banana, and Almond Milk; 33
- **Lunch:** Lentil Soup; 53
- **Dinner:** Garlic and Herb Roasted Chicken; 74

Day 13

- **Breakfast:** Mushroom and Swiss Cheese Omelet; 34
- **Lunch:** Chicken and Veggie Stir-Fry; 54
- **Dinner:** Vegetarian Chili; 75

Day 14

- **Breakfast:** Low-Carb Pancakes with Almond Flour; 34
- **Lunch:** Caprese Salad with Balsamic Glaze; 54
- **Dinner:** Pesto Zoodle Bowl with Cherry Tomatoes; 75

Day 15

- **Breakfast:** Scrambled Eggs with Smoked Salmon; 35
- **Lunch:** Tuna Salad Lettuce Wraps; 55
- **Dinner:** Turkey and Zucchini Lasagna; 76

Day 16

- **Breakfast:** Zucchini and Tomato Frittata; 35
- **Lunch:** Greek Salad with Feta Cheese; 55
- **Dinner:** Chicken Piccata; 76

Day 17

- **Breakfast:** Green Smoothie with Kale and Avocado; 36
- **Lunch:** Stuffed Bell Peppers with Quinoa; 56
- **Dinner:** Eggplant Parmesan; 77

Day 18

- **Breakfast:** Baked Avocado with Egg; 36
- **Lunch:** Spinach and Chicken Caesar Wrap; 56
- **Dinner:** Mushroom and Chicken Risotto; 78

Day 19

- **Breakfast:** Turkey Bacon and Egg Breakfast Sandwich; 37
- **Lunch:** Asian Chicken Lettuce Wraps; 57
- **Dinner:** Salmon and Avocado Salad; 79

Day 20

- **Breakfast:** Quinoa Breakfast Bowl with Berries; 37
- **Lunch:** Balsamic Chicken and Vegetables; 57
- **Dinner:** Beef and Vegetable Kabobs; 79

Day 21

- **Breakfast:** Ricotta Cheese with Fresh Raspberries; 38
- **Lunch:** Tomato Basil Soup; 58
- **Dinner:** Turkey Meatloaf with Cauliflower Mash; 80

Day 22

- **Breakfast:** Pumpkin Spice Chia Pudding; 38
- **Lunch:** Eggplant Rollatini; 58
- **Dinner:** Stuffed Cabbage Rolls; 81

Day 23

- **Breakfast:** Protein Pancakes with Greek Yogurt; 39
- **Lunch:** Kale and Quinoa Salad; 59
- **Dinner:** Roasted Turkey Breast with Brussels Sprouts; 81

Day 24

- **Breakfast:** Low-Carb Bagel with Cream Cheese and Cucumber; 39
- **Lunch:** Chicken and Avocado Salad; 59
- **Dinner:** Zucchini and Ground Beef Skillet; 82

Day 25

- **Breakfast:** Berry and Spinach Smoothie; 40
- **Lunch:** Turkey Chili; 60
- **Dinner:** Roasted Lemon Herb Chicken; 82

Day 26

- **Breakfast:** Cauliflower Hash Browns; 40
- **Lunch:** Grilled Salmon Salad; 60
- **Dinner:** Broiled Swordfish with Citrus Salsa; 83

Day 27

- **Breakfast:** Mango and Coconut Chia Pudding; 41
- **Lunch:** Chicken and Broccoli Alfredo; 61
- **Dinner:** Baked Eggplant with Tomato Sauce; 84

Day 28

- **Breakfast:** Stuffed Bell Peppers with Eggs; 41
- **Lunch:** Turkey and Zucchini Skillet; 61
- **Dinner:** Shrimp Scampi with Zucchini Noodles; 84

Day 29

- **Breakfast:** Green Tea Smoothie with Matcha; 42
- **Lunch:** Sweet Potato and Black Bean Tacos; 62
- **Dinner:** Thai Peanut Chicken with Veggie Noodles; 85

Day 30

- **Breakfast:** Cinnamon and Apple Oatmeal; 42
- **Lunch:** Baked Cod with Asparagus; 62
- **Dinner:** Garlic Butter Shrimp and Veggie Foil Packets; 86

This 30-day meal plan provides a variety of delicious and nutritious meals, ensuring that you enjoy a balanced diet while managing your diabetes effectively. Each meal is carefully selected to provide essential nutrients and maintain stable blood sugar levels. Enjoy your healthy and flavorful journey!

Recipe Index

Conclusion

Congratulations on taking the first steps towards better health and well-being with "Diabetic Diet After 50:1900+ Days of Easy, Low-Carb, Low-Sugar Healthy Recipes – The Complete Cookbook with Delicious Food and 30-Day Meal Plan for Senior Diabetics and Health-Conscious Individuals." This journey is about more than just managing diabetes; it's about embracing a lifestyle that promotes overall wellness, vitality, and longevity.

Variety and Enjoyment

Eating healthily doesn't mean sacrificing flavor or enjoyment. With over 1900 days of diverse, delicious recipes, you have the opportunity to explore new foods, flavors, and cooking techniques. From hearty breakfasts and wholesome lunches to nutritious dinners and guilt-free desserts, each meal can be a delightful experience that supports your health goals.

Practical Strategies

The practical tips for meal planning, grocery shopping, and cooking equip you with the skills to incorporate healthy eating into your daily routine seamlessly. Whether it's understanding food labels, identifying hidden sugars and carbs, or mastering portion control and meal timing, these strategies are designed to make your dietary journey easier and more sustainable.

Long-Term Health Benefits

Adopting a healthy diabetic diet has numerous long-term benefits. It can enhance your energy levels, improve mental clarity, and support emotional well-being. Most importantly, it helps you manage diabetes effectively, reducing the risk of complications and improving your overall quality of life.

Community and Support

Remember, you are not alone on this journey. Share your experiences, recipes, and successes with friends, family, and support groups. Encouraging others to join you in healthy eating can create a supportive community that fosters better health for everyone.

Commitment to Health

Committing to your health is a powerful step. By choosing to follow the guidelines and recipes in this book, you are prioritizing your well-being and setting a positive example for others. Every meal is an opportunity to nourish your body, mind, and spirit.

Final Thoughts

Thank you for allowing this book to be a part of your health journey. May it serve as a valuable resource and inspiration as you navigate the path to better health. Embrace the variety, savor the flavors, and enjoy the many benefits of a healthy diabetic diet. Here's to a future filled with vitality, joy, and well-being!

Wishing you health and happiness, Jakob Stivenson.

Made in United States
Troutdale, OR
11/11/2024

24690286R00060